ESCAPE FROM PAGANISM

How a Roman Catholic Can Be Saved.

LARRY BALL

Trafford
PUBLISHING®

Escape From Paganism
www.EscapeFromPaganism.com

Order this book online at www.trafford.com/08-0203
or email orders@trafford.com

Most Trafford titles are also available at major online book retailers.

© Copyright 2008 Larry Ball.

All rights reserved. No part of this publication may be reproduced, stored in a retrieval system, or transmitted, in any form or by any means, electronic, mechanical, photocopying, recording, or otherwise, without the written prior permission of the author except in the case of brief quotations embodied in critical articles or reviews.

TX6-862-397

Cover and interior design: Robert Greuter & Associates.
All Scripture quotations are taken from the Revised Standard Version.

Note for Librarians: A cataloguing record for this book is available from Library and Archives Canada at www.collectionscanada.ca/amicus/index-e.html

ISBN: 978-1-4251-7128-5

We at Trafford believe that it is the responsibility of us all, as both individuals and corporations, to make choices that are environmentally and socially sound. You, in turn, are supporting this responsible conduct each time you purchase a Trafford book, or make use of our publishing services. To find out how you are helping, please visit www.trafford.com/responsiblepublishing.html

Our mission is to efficiently provide the world's finest, most comprehensive book publishing service, enabling every author to experience success. To find out how to publish your book, your way, and have it available worldwide, visit us online at www.trafford.com/10510

Trafford
PUBLISHING

www.trafford.com

North America & international
toll-free: 1 888 232 4444 (USA & Canada)
phone: 250 383 6864 ♦ fax: 250 383 6804
email: info@trafford.com

The United Kingdom & Europe
phone: +44 (0)1865 487 395 ♦ local rate: 0845 230 9601
facsimile: +44 (0)1865 481 507 ♦ email: info.uk@trafford.com

10 9 8 7 6 5 4 3 2

CONTENTS

Preface 7
Death 13
What Is the Imagery We See Today? 17
Their Eyes Were Opened 23
Murder Based Upon Religion 27
Enmity and Wrath 31
Can One Avoid Death? 35
Roman Catholic World View 39
Council of Constance .43
Saint Bartholomew's Day Massacre 49
Altar Footstool 53
Kidnapping of Edgardo Mortara 57
Is the Pope the Supreme Ruler of the World? 61
Summary 67
God's World View 71
God Is Boss 75
The Alpha and Omega 81
God Has Spoken through the Apostles 85
God's Word Is Complete 89
Biblical Proof That The Roman Church Is Pagan 93
Is Man God? 99
The Clay's War with The Potter 105
Vicar of Christ 111
The Sacraments 119
What Is Grace? 125

CONTENTS

New Law 129
Sacrament of Baptism 133
Sacrament of Penance 145
Sacrament of Confirmation 155
Extreme Unction 159
Eucharist Mass 169
The Wafer God 179
Cannibalism? 183
Dung! 187
Sacrament of Orders 191
Examination Time 195
The Real Church 203
It Is Sunday About 2,000 Years Ago 207
Just What Is Happening? 211
The Mystery 217
The Rock 221
Jesus Christ, the One Sacrifice 229
The Universal Church Versus the Local Church 235
Tradition, Scripture, and The "Authority" of
The Roman Church 245
Let's Give This Stuff A "Sherlocking" 251
Tradition 257
Did The Orthodox Fathers Sanction Tradition
Over Scripture? 263
Does The Roman Church Have Sole Authority
For Interpreting Scripture? 269
Jabberwocky and Gobbledegook 275
The Virgin Mary or Goddess Myrionymus,
(Ishtar) Queen of Heaven, The Woman
with a Thousand Names? 279

CONTENTS

What Did Christ Say About Mary's Role? 283
Mary Myth Manifested 287
Mary, Mother Of God 293
Mary Queen of Heaven 299
The Fable Continues 303
The Immaculate Conception 307
Mary, the Perpetual Virgin .313
A Wild West Story, Well, Almost. The Death
and Assumption of Mary 317
Mary's Dominion in Heaven,
or is it Domineering Heaven? 323
Mary's Little Godlets, the Saints 329
Shrouded in Fantasy 335
Some Absolutely Incredible Saints 339
The Godlets 343
From Whence Came the Idea of Saints 347
Did You Know? 351
The Hot Spot: Purgatory 355
A History of the Concept of Purgatory 359
The Credibility of The Creeds 369
You Can Be Sure of Your Salvation 373
A Parade 377
Human Sacrifice Was Common 381
"Christianity" Legitimized By Emperor Constantine . .385
Yet Another Parade 389
The Great White Throne Judgment 395
The Judgment 399
Victory In Jesus 405
Appendix: Successors of Peter? Really? 411

Preface

Why did I write this book? Is not the answer to this question the purpose of all book "prefaces?"

The title is provocative and labels Roman Catholicism as Pagan and not Christian. Am I trying to pick on Roman Catholics? Why *did* I write this book?

Go back with me to the spring of 1971. I was an agnostic making my own way, and did not need God, whom I really did not think existed anyway. Think about that word "agnostic." It is a compound word that means without knowledge. In the sense that I have used it, it means without knowledge of God.

When you think about being without knowledge of God, you have to think of the condition, "atheoi." What is this? It is the Greek word from which we derive the word "atheist." It means to be without God. To be an agnostic is to be an atheist, because if you are without knowledge of Him, you are without Him.

So what has this to do with Roman Catholicism? Just this, the Roman Church is **atheistic**. Atheistic? Do they not believe in the God of the Bible, His Son, Jesus Christ and the Holy Spirit, the Triune God?

"Well," you might respond, "they sure do, they are always speaking about them! Your statement is false!"

Now we are at the purpose of this book. This book will prove with a resounding **no**; they do not believe in the God of the Bible or His Son the Lord Jesus Christ. As you will see, the Roman Church does not believe in the Bible as **the** revelation of God. They add to it "Tradition and the Magisterium" of the Church. In fact, when you look at their rituals and catechism (which this book covers) you will see that they believe in many gods and in their catechism **damns** the real God.

If you are Roman Catholic, you are, then, agnostic and atheist. This is not meant as a slur upon you or any Roman Catholic.

It is merely stating that you are in the same condition I was in, back in 1971. I was without the knowledge of and the companionship of the Living God. This book is meant as a rescue call.

Back in 1971, I received a rescue call. A friend talked to me about Christ and my need for Him as my Savior. I insulted him but he kept it up for six months. He finally asked me if I had ever read the Bible. I told him no, I had not, but often thought I should so I could show people like him how silly it was.

He challenged me to read the Bible, so I bought one and started reading at Genesis 1 (he had recommended the Gospel of John) and read to Genesis 25. By this point I had become well acquainted with a man described as a friend of God, Abraham. But Abraham was a sinner, a terrible sinner in my mind, but so was I. God, though, saved Abraham and declared him righteous. By this point I was under the conviction of the Holy Spirit. I knew that in my own way, I was as big a sinner as was Abraham. If God could save Abraham, maybe He would save me.

Finally, in my office one day, I closed the door and took out a tract that had a prayer in it. Before I said it I asked God to help me in my unbelief. Then I prayed to receive Christ as my Savior. My life began to change! I had been rescued from the path to Hell and was given eternal life.

Assured eternal life! No loss of salvation each time I committed a sin as I was born into God's family and would be disciplined by Him from within. No need to confess to a priest my sins as they were continually being confessed through the Holy Spirit. No need to sacrifice Christ over and over again in the mass as His one sacrifice on the cross was sufficient – according to His own words. He said "it is over." No purgatory was needed to clean me up, as the Holy Spirit within is perfecting me. When I die, I will be perfect and present with the Lord— **not** because of what I do to clean up my act, but because of what God is doing to clean me up from the inside out.

We will look at all of these issues and more within this book. I have used the Roman Catechism of Trent, which was reaffirmed by Vatican II. Many other historical sources, all documented in the book, were used. I would recommend that you have a Bible handy as you read this book and make sure of what I am stating; it can be eternally important.

Salvation for those who are "agnostic/atheistic," in other words, without knowledge and the companionship of the living God of the Bible, is the purpose of this book. It **is** possible to know that you are saved and saved forever without end or hiccup.

There is an old hymn entitled, *Throw out the lifeline.* Please approach this book with that thought in mind. This book is intended as a lifeline, to provide information for the rescue of those that are perishing.

—Larry Ball, 2008

Death

Have you noticed that the newspapers are filled with stories of death – death in accidents, death in war, death in terrorist activities, and the special death pages entitled "obituaries?" Then consider your own family – how far back can you go until your ancestors are all dead? Do you have a great-grandparent, or a great-great grandparent still living? The generations of man die off pretty quickly.

Have you ever considered how and why death started? It started with our original ancestor, Adam, and his wife, Eve. Get out your Bible and open it to Genesis chapter 1. This is the account of God's creation of "all." There are a few things that I want to call to your attention.

> And God created man in his own image, in the image of God created he him; male and female created he them. And God blessed them: and God said unto them, Be fruitful, and multiply, and replenish the earth, and subdue it; and have dominion over the fish of the sea, and over the birds of the heavens, and over every living thing that moveth upon the earth. And God said, Behold, I have given you every herb yielding seed, which is upon the face of all the earth, and every tree, in which is the fruit of a tree yielding seed; to you it shall be for food: and to every beast of the earth, and to every bird of the heavens, and to everything that creepeth upon the earth, wherein there is life, I have given every green herb for food: and it was so. And God saw everything that he had made, and, behold, it was very good (Genesis 1:27-31 ASV).

Man was created in the **image of God**. What does this mean? Well, it doesn't mean that when you look into the mirror you see an image of God looking back at you, because God is Spirit. What the meaning does include is the moral and righteous character of God.

Man was created by God as someone special. God **blessed** man, which means he was in a state of happiness, prosperity, free from want, free from harm, free from fear, in a state of bliss. Wouldn't that be a wonderful way to live?

"In the image of God" describes what a man is. By "man" is meant "male and female He created them" (Genesis 1:27). He was created **very good** - body, spirit, soul, and image. A better translation of verse 1:27 is that God created man *as* His own image. Man's purpose was to be God's image bearer upon the earth.

Notice that the image of God is a constituent part of man. Without the image, man is not man. The image is part of man's nature. It is as much a part of man as is his mouth and head, or his arms, legs, and torso. You cannot take the image of God from man and still have man be man.

Another important aspect of man (Adam) is his status. "Status" means his position in regard to law. What law? The law, or rule of God is the intention, or purpose, for which God created all things. Man was created **good.** In this regard, "good" signifies righteous. God created Adam good, and this placed Adam in the state or status of righteousness. Adam was created righteous or just. He had to be if he was to bear the image of God in his dominion over the earth (vv. 1:28-30) and act within the will of God.

Understand that "righteousness" and "just" are forensic or juristic terms. That means they are legal or law terms. They define a man's actions from a legal viewpoint. They do not define his physical, spiritual, or soul makeup. (Consider this aspect very carefully as it will come up later when salvation is considered. There is at least one great heresy practiced today that relates to this.)

Man had the right to live and exercise such character over his domain, and therefore rule with moral goodness, exhibiting the will and image of God to creation. Man had it made.

God's creation was so good that He took a rest (see Genesis 2:1-3). God rested from His work of creation - and rests to this day. His work was perfect; no further "creation" has been needed. He does, however "recreate."

What Is the Imagery We See Today?

When we look around us today, we do not see this imagery, do we? Man lives in fear of sickness, injury, habitation, starvation, natural disaster, war, and a host of other perils that lead to death. Man is enslaved to the fear of death (see Hebrews 2:13). What happened to the blessing God placed upon man?

God placed man in the Garden of Eden. The trees in the garden bore fruit and man was told to eat freely from all the trees except from the Tree of the Knowledge of Good and Evil, for if they did, they would truly die (see Genesis 2:17).

It is not long before a rather "charming" character comes to visit the woman.

> Now the serpent was more subtle than any beast of the field which Jehovah God had made. And he said unto the woman, Yea, hath God said, Ye shall not eat of any tree of the garden? And the woman said unto the serpent, Of the fruit of the trees of the garden we may eat: but of the fruit of the tree which is in the midst of the garden, God hath said, Ye shall not eat of it, neither shall ye touch it, lest ye die. And the serpent said unto the woman, Ye shall not surely die: for God doth know that in the day ye eat thereof, then your eyes shall be opened, and ye shall be as God, knowing good and evil. And when the woman saw that the tree was good for food, and that it was a delight to the eyes, and that the tree was to be desired to make one wise, she took of the fruit thereof, and did eat; and she gave also unto her husband with her, and he did eat. And the eyes of them both were opened, and they knew that they were naked; and they sewed fig-leaves together, and made themselves aprons (Genesis 3:1-7 ASV).

Look at the essence of the serpent's sales pitch; then look at the woman's thought process:

The serpent (identified as Satan in Scripture):

You will **not** surely **die;**

He goes on and infers that God is withholding something from her. If you eat:

> Your **eyes** will be **opened,**
>
> You will **become** as **God,**
>
> You will know **good** from **evil.**

Remember the summation of God's creative work? It was **very good.** Man was in charge, and he was blessed. Man was not subject to death (calamity, sorrow or fear). He had it made. God protected him. Man knew **good** and did not know **evil. Good only!** Why would he want to know evil?

Yet, here we have the serpent (Satan) casting doubt upon the **Word of God** (this Word was Scripture for Adam and Eve; it was their Bible). Note how cunningly the serpent said God is a liar.

Now look at the woman's reaction: She saw that the tree was good for food, that it was pleasant to the eyes, and a tree desirable to make one wise; she took of its fruit and ate.

Her reaction defines the roots of sin for man for all time:

> The tree was good for food – the **lust** of the flesh.
>
> It was pleasant to the eyes – the **lust** of the eyes.
>
> It would make one wise – the **boastful pride** of life.

These three lusts have been labeled as the **Triune God** of the natural man, it equates to **me, myself, and I.** (See 1 John 2:16 for more on these lusts.)

Then she gave to the man, and he ate. The man was the person to whom God spoke when He gave the prohibition against eating from this particular tree. It is the only prohibition placed upon man by God. Since the man had received the Word directly from the mouth of God, the man had the greater responsibility to obey it.

However, the man did not obey God. He also subjected himself to the lusts of sin and took from the woman, in rebellion against God. After all, had not the Serpent told them that if they ate from the Tree they would become as God? What was there to worry about? They soon found out.

Remember, God created man **as** His own image. Look at the three motives for sin again. Adam was only the **image** of God. Satan pointed out that they could **become God** by eating from the forbidden tree. Why would Adam want to submit to God as only His image when he, too, could be God and determine himself what was good and what was evil? His pride and lust took over, and he also ate from the tree.

Man still bears the image of God, because it is part of man. Again, without the image, man is not man. From this point on, though, man in Adam, **perverts the image of God and uses it against God.** Man is at war with God. That is why man's nature is sinful, and every one of us sins. Man at this point becomes an enemy of the "State." Man lost his "status" of righteousness. Man is an **outlaw** to the "State" or "Status" established by God.

Man, under God's law, is a criminal in rebellion against God. Man's mind is the mind of the flesh, not of the Spirit. His natural bent, from here on out, is to use the "image" of God against God. All of Adam's descendents will act this way. From this, then, man is naturally inclined to commit crimes and each is individually guilty of crimes against God. From the aspect of man's nature and actions, he has no hope. His righteousness is gone. He has to die. Death is the reward of sin.

Concisely, then, here is the nature of man:

- He bears the image of God.
- All men are in a state of enmity (rebellion) against God, by their very nature – (all men sin and are born in sin, because of Adam).
- Man is guilty of his crimes before God.
- Man has a penalty to pay – "the wages of sin are death" (Romans 6:23).
- Man is lost.

Their Eyes Were Opened

And the eyes of them both were opened, and they knew that they were naked; and they sewed fig-leaves together, and made themselves aprons (Genesis 3:7 ASV).

Something happened: "Their eyes were opened!" They saw that they were naked. I imagine that in you, as me, this thought, even now conjures up some discomfort. They now had thoughts, fears, phobias, that were evil. These thoughts did not exist just moments before, as they were innocent and lived in innocent bliss – blessed by God. But they rejected God's blessing; they rejected God, thinking that they would become God.

Having rejected God, they now feared Him and hid from His fellowship.

> And they heard the voice of Jehovah God walking in the garden in the cool of the day: and the man and his wife hid themselves from the presence of Jehovah God amongst the trees of the garden (Genesis 3:8 ASV).

But God sought man out. He called to Adam, "Where are you?" (v. 9).

The summary of a trial is recorded in Genesis 3:10-24; God held court right there in the garden.

Adam's Testimony: "I heard thy voice in the garden, and I was afraid, because I was naked; and I hid myself" (v. 10).

God's Question: "Who told thee that thou wast naked? Hast thou eaten of the tree, whereof I commanded thee that thou shouldest not eat?" (v. 11).

Adam's Evasive Answer: "The woman whom thou gavest to be with me, she gave me of the tree, and I did eat" (v. 12).

Note Adam's "manliness." In his answer, he shows his guilt, and then he shifts the blame to God. It is God's fault for giving him that woman! The inference here is that Adam is ready to sacrifice her also. I am sure you have seen people use this strategy when in trouble. How about you? Have you ever been in so much trouble that you would try to shift blame or implicate someone else? Kids do it all the time. Isn't the whole theory of "plea bargaining" for the cooperation of a criminal based upon this concept? Man is weak and it all started right here with Adam.

The woman answers God's question honestly, as it is supported in the New Testament as being true. The woman stated that her motivation was because she was deceived by the serpent. That is true although her actions were motivated by the forces of sin, the three lusts.

DEATH'S REWARD

The result of this trial is that God places a curse upon the serpent and puts enmity between the serpent and the woman. The result of this enmity will be that the woman will bear a child that will be injured by the serpent, but that this child will destroy the serpent. The child will be of the seed of the woman. This particular description purposely leaves out a man's participation in the conception of a child. It refers to the virgin birth of Christ (see v. 3:15). We now know that the **seed** of woman was bruised; He died upon a cross, but rose again, and that the serpent, Satan, will someday be crushed and thrown into the Lake of Fire forever.

God then pronounced the sentence upon the woman and Adam. He told Adam, "You [will] return to the ground, for out of it you were taken; for dust you are and to dust you shall return" (Genesis 3:19 ASV). Adam will die; so all will surely die.

Adam and Eve are driven out of the Garden to certain death. It is a death that is tinged with mercy for Adam and Eve. Since they had knowledge of good and evil if they ate from the Tree of Life they would live forever with that knowledge. We have seen that the knowledge of evil produces sin. To live forever in their sin would not be to their advantage or to God's purpose.

Murder Based Upon Religion

The first recorded physical human death is a murder. Cain, the first-born from Adam and Eve, murdered his brother Abel. Later comes another killing. Lamech, the grandson of Cain, also kills a man. This is the second human death recorded in the Bible. You can read this account in Genesis 4.

We need to consider what death is. We know it when we see it, don't we? A motionless, lifeless body is a dead body, correct? Sure it is. But so is a person who is spiritually separated from God. That person is spiritually lifeless, spiritually dead.

We see this in Cain. He has contact with God up to the point that God casts him away for refusing to humble himself to God and murdering Abel.

> And now cursed art thou from the ground, which hath opened its mouth to receive thy brother's blood from thy hand; when thou tillest the ground, it shall not henceforth yield unto thee its strength; a fugitive and a wanderer shalt thou be in the earth. And Cain said unto Jehovah, My punishment is greater than I can bear. Behold, thou hast driven me out this day from the face of the ground; and from thy face shall I be hid; and I shall be a fugitive and a wanderer in the earth; and it will come to pass, that whosoever findeth me will slay me (Genesis 4: 11-14 ASV).

Cain was subjected to spiritual death – separation from God is death. God cast Cain off to be alone in the world, separated from God. "My punishment is greater than I can bear!" Cain cried. He was spiritually dead; someday he would be physically dead and will suffer the second death, the Lake of Fire. Indeed, he placed himself in deep trouble. He will bear this penalty into and throughout eternity.

Cain had no further direct contact with God. God hid his face from Cain. Cain was dead, even though he was still breathing.

Incidentally, according to the Book of Revelation, the guilt of this crime, Cain slaying Abel, will be laid at the feet of Babylon the great at the end of the 70th week of Daniel or the

Tribulation period, which is yet future. Cain's actions were the chief cornerstone of all the false religious systems since his time.

> And in her was found the blood of prophets and of saints, and of all that have been slain upon the earth" (Revelation 18:24 ASV).

Enmity and Wrath

Chapter 5 of Genesis contains a series of obituaries. Adam's death is recorded, then Adam's son, Seth, then Adam's grandson, Enosh, then Adam's great-grandson, Kenan and on for eight generations. All died.

> And Jehovah saw that the wickedness of man was great in the earth, and that every imagination of the thoughts of his heart was only evil continually (Genesis 6:5 ASV).

Because of this, God determined to destroy man with a flood (see Genesis 7). Only eight people survived the flood: Noah, and his family. Some have calculated that there may have been up to two-billion people on the earth at that time, and all but eight perished.

Think about it; everyone died. Even without a flood everyone dies. Noah and his family eventually all died. All of us die.

> Therefore, as through one man sin entered into the world, and death through sin; and so death passed unto all men, for that all sinned (Romans 5:12).

Scripture says "all sinned." From Adam and Eve right down to you and me, all have sinned and were born in sin. All of us, in Adam, are in a state of rebellion against God – a state of enmity. Any time God's Word says something, and you do different, you are at enmity with God. Further, because of man's rebellion, man is in a state of enmity against all other men.

God, too, was at enmity with man and exercised His wrath.

> For the wrath of God is revealed from heaven against all ungodliness and unrighteousness of men, who hinder the truth in unrighteousness; because that which is known of God is manifest in them; for God manifested it unto them. For the invisible things of him since the creation of the world are clearly seen, being perceived through the things that are made, even his everlasting power and divinity; that they may be without excuse: because that, knowing God, they glorified him not as God, neither gave thanks; but became vain in their reasonings, and their senseless heart was darkened. Professing themselves to be wise,

they became fools, and changed the glory of the incorruptible God for the likeness of an image of corruptible man, and of birds, and four-footed beasts, and creeping things.

Wherefore God gave them up in the lusts of their hearts unto uncleanness, that their bodies should be dishonored among themselves: for that they exchanged the truth of God for a lie, and worshipped and served the creature rather than the Creator, who is blessed for ever. Amen. For this cause God gave them up unto vile passions: for their women changed the natural use into that which is against nature: and likewise also the men, leaving the natural use of the woman, burned in their lust one toward another, men with men working unseemliness, and receiving in themselves that recompense of their error which was due. And even as they refused to have God in their knowledge, God gave them up unto a reprobate mind, to do those things which are not fitting; being filled with all unrighteousness, wickedness, covetousness, maliciousness; full of envy, murder, strife, deceit, malignity; whisperers, backbiters, hateful to God, insolent, haughty, boastful, inventors of evil things, disobedient to parents, without understanding, covenant-breakers, without natural affection, unmerciful: who, knowing the ordinance of God, that they that practice such things are worthy of death, not only do the same, but also consent with them that practice them (Romans 1:18-32 ASV).

Man, at this point is in big trouble – but is there hope or help?

Can One Avoid Death?

There are three aspects or types of death: spiritual, physical, and eternal. All are considered death because each one is separated from God. Without God, there is no life.

We have discussed physical and spiritual death, but we need to consider one other aspect of death – eternal death. The Book of Revelation calls this the second death. The second death is eternal.

> Then Death and Hades were cast into the Lake of Fire. This is the second death. And anyone not found written in the Book of Life was cast into the lake of fire (Revelation 20:14, 15).

This is the death that our Lord describes as outer darkness, where there is weeping and gnashing of teeth, where the "worm" does not die. It is death with awareness. It is a death of constant and eternal suffering. **It is a death we can avoid.** That is good news.

To come to this Good News, however, we will have to examine two world views: man's and God's. Both claim to be the "way" to the Good News. Remember, Cain was the chief cornerstone of man's solution to this problem. His solution failed. We will consider a representation of man's views: the Roman Catholic World View, then God's. After this we will compare the requirements of each.

Roman Catholic World View

MSNBC News Services
Updated 8:52 a.m. CT, Tues., July 10, 2007

    LORENZAGO DI CADORE, Italy. Pope Benedict XVI has reasserted the universal primacy of the Roman Catholic Church, approving a document released Tuesday that says Orthodox churches were defective and that other Christian denominations were not true churches.

    It restates key sections of a 2000 document the pope wrote when he was prefect of the congregation, "Dominus Iesus," which set off a firestorm of criticism among Protestant and other Christian denominations because it said they were not true churches but merely ecclesial communities and therefore did not have the "means of salvation."

    In the new document and an accompanying commentary, which were released as the pope vacations here in Italy's Dolomite Mountains, the Vatican repeated that position.

    "Christ 'established here on earth' only one church," the document said. The other communities "cannot be called 'churches' in the proper sense" because they do not have apostolic succession — the ability to trace their bishops back to Christ's original apostles

With this news release, Pope Benedict XVI, depicts a little of the Roman Catholic World View.

What happens to you when you die? Will you go to heaven or hell? The Pope, in the news release above, clearly states that if you are not a Roman Catholic your destination is hell.

What authority does the Pope have to make this statement? It is called "Papal primacy." Papal primacy was established at the Council of Florence. This council was held at Florence (Firenze), Italy between the years 1431-35 AD.

What is Papal primacy? It is derived from what they teach is "apostolic succession." The Roman Church claims apostolic succession from the Apostle Peter. The Roman Church also claims that the church was founded upon Peter and that he was the first pope. The scriptural basis of this claim is their interpretation of the Gospel of Matthew 16:13-19 (ASV):

> Now when Jesus came into the parts of Caesarea Philippi, he asked his disciples, saying, Who do men say that the Son of man is? And they said, Some say John the Baptist; some, Elijah; and others, Jeremiah, or one of the prophets. He saith unto them, But who say ye that I am? And Simon Peter answered and said, Thou art the Christ, the Son of the living God. And Jesus answered and said unto him, Blessed art thou, Simon Bar-Jonah: for flesh and blood hath not revealed it unto thee, but my Father who is in heaven. And I also say unto thee, that thou art Peter, and upon this rock I will build my church; and the gates of Hades shall not prevail against it. I will give unto thee the keys of the kingdom of heaven: and whatsoever thou shalt bind on earth shall be bound in heaven; and whatsoever thou shalt loose on earth shall be loosed in heaven.

The Roman Church claims direct succession for the Pope from the Apostle Peter and all the powers that they claim Christ gave to Peter in the statement above.

> In this Church of Christ the Roman Pontiff, as the successor of Peter, to whom Christ entrusted the care of his sheep and his lambs, has been granted by God supreme, full, immediate and universal power in the care of souls. He is endowed with the primacy of power over all the churches (Vatican Council II, Volume 1, *The Conciliar and the Post Conciliar Documents,* Austin Flannery, O.P.).

The above statement from Vatican II is pretty comprehensive. Since their claim to the primacy of the Pope goes back to the 1400s, let's look at some historical expressions of this power and then some theological assertions about final authority, which means "who is boss?" Before we do, however, consider the two following definitions. Keeping them in mind will help you understand the Roman Church's World View.

> **What is papal primacy?** Papal primacy is the concept that the bishop of Rome (the pope) is the universal pastor and supreme head of the Catholic Church. He has full, supreme, immediate, and universal jurisdictional authority to govern the church. This means that no bishop, synod, or council of bishops can override his authority. His teach-

ing authority is defined as the doctrine of papal infallibility. His governing authority is contained in papal primacy.

What is papal infallibility? Papal infallibility is a dogma solemnly defined at the First Vatican Council (1869-1870). Vatican II in Lumen Gentium #25, Canon 749 of the 1983 Code of Canon Law and the Catechism #891 explain the doctrine: "By virtue of his office, the Roman Pontiff possesses infallibility in teaching when as the supreme pastor and teacher of all the Christian faithful, who strengthens his brothers, and sisters in the faith, he proclaims by definitive act that a doctrine of faith or morals is to be held." This charisma (gift) of infallibility is exercised only when the Pope issues an ex cathedra statement on faith and morals or when he proposes a teaching united with all the bishops of the world (*The Catholic Answer Book,* Rev. John Trigilio Jr., Th.d. & Rev. Kenneth Brighenti, Ph.d., pages 310-311)

You need to understand this "ex cathedra" issue. Anytime the Pope speaks "ex cathedra" they claim the Holy Spirit has hold of him and is dictating what he says. In the addendum of this book is a list of scurrilous popes, murderers, non-celibate men siring illegitimate children, admitted unbelievers, heretics, thieves, and even one pirate. These men and one woman lived sinful lives, but when they sat in the "chair" (ex cathedra), the Holy Spirit supposedly took control and the words of God came forth. This is abominable and a direct attack on the character and person of God.

Council of Constance

The **Council of Constance** (Kontanz) took place just a few years before the Council of Florence. The city of Kontanz is about 27 miles northeast of Zurich, Switzerland. This council was held between the years of 1414-18 AD. Its accomplishments were the condemnation of Wycliff, Hus, and the ending of a Papal schism (there were three active popes at the time). This council restored the unity of the Catholic religion by bringing it back under the authority of one pope.

We are going to examine the story of the condemnation and burning of Jon Hus. It is from this story that the Roman Church has set forth a declaration of its supreme authority in the world.

The story begins in the late 1300s in England. John Wycliff, a priest and a professor at Oxford University, translated the Bible into English and launched some severe criticisms of the Roman Church, charging, among other things, that the Pope was anti-Christ. At the time the King of England was married to a Princess of Bohemia (currently the Czech Republic.) There was quite a bit of interaction between the two kingdoms.

In 1406, after the death of John Wycliff, some of his teachings spread to Bohemia. A professor/priest at Prague by the name of Jon Hus began teaching and expanding on them. This caused great turmoil, but as Hus had the backing of the King, he was allowed to continue. The Archbishop of Prague, however, excommunicated Hus and his followers in 1410 AD, the result of which Hus was summoned to appear before Pope John XXIII at Rome. Hus, under the protection of the King, begged off.

In 1414 AD, a council of the Roman Church was urged by Sigismund, the Emperor of the Holy Roman Empire. Among the problems he urged the church to address were the issues raised by Hus. The Emperor had given Hus a safe conduct pass to attend and debate the council. The Roman Church, after hearing Hus, thought otherwise and an historic position was taken that the Church's word, or promise, did not and could not be honored on behalf of a heretic. Consequently, they condemned and burned Jon Hus at the stake in July, 1415 AD.

What is the position of the Church and the Pope on its word or commitment? (The Bishop of Rome is the Pope.)

If we turn to the Canon Law of Rome, which comprises the decrees and bulls of Popes, we find the following statements:

- The Bishop of Rome has power to absolve from allegiance, obligation, bond of service, promise, and compact, the provinces, cities, and armies of kings that rebel against him, and also to loose their [citizens] (Clementin, lib ii, tit. I, cap ii).
- The Bishop of Rome may excommunicate emperors and princes, depose them from their states and assoil their subjects from their oath of obedience to them (Corpus Juris Canonici, Decreti, pars. I., distinct xcvi, can x., and Decreti, para. Ii, cause xv., quest. Vi. Can. Iii, iv., v.).
- The pontifical authority absolves some from their oath of allegiance (Corpus Juris Canonici, Decreti. Pars ii, causa xv., quest vi. Can iii).
- An oath sworn against the good of the Church does not bind; because that is not an oath, but a perjury rather, which is taken against the Church's interests (Decreti Gregorii, lib. Ii, tit. xxiv., cap. xxvii.).

Pope Pius IX (who was beatified by John Paul), in a "Syllabus of Errors" issued in 1864, declared that the Church, or Canon Law is above and not subject to civil authority, that is, the Priest is above the State. The following points are taken from *Is the Roman Church Holy?* By H.A. Henderson and Chas. J. Thynne.

- Kings and princes and citizens were subject to the Roman Catholic Church.
- It was wicked to allow Protestants equal rights with Roman Catholics.
- That the Bishop of Rome (the Pope) can be judged only by God (Decret. Pars ii., cause iii, quest vi, can ix.).
- A Pope is the absolute judge of his own actions, in all circumstances, and that he could annul the promises he had previously made (*Cormenin's History,* 2, 111).
- Innocent III laid down the proud maxim that out of the fullness of his power, he might lawfully dispense with the law (*Europe During the Middle Ages,* by Hallam, p. 373).

In the burning of Hus and dishonoring the promise of safe travel, Rome was merely acting within the prerogatives of its Canon law. This is law that is still in effect today.

Saint Bartholomew's Day Massacre

In Paris, France, August 24, 1572, a conspiracy by and between the Queen Mother of France, Catherine de Medici, the King of France, the heir apparent, his brother, French Catholic leadership, the Spanish government, and Pope Gregory XIII at the Vatican, French Catholics were incited to rise up and slaughter the French Calvinists, known as Huguenauts.

At least 100,000 defenseless men, women, and children were massacred in one day. The rivers of France were filled with dead bodies. Thousands of Huguenauts, not slaughtered were imprisoned. Many were enslaved by the French government to serve out the rest of their lives as galley slaves.

The day is remembered as the Saint Bartholomew's Day Massacre. Pope Gregory was so enthralled at this "heroic action" that he had a special medal made in honor of it. Further, he had Georgi Vasari, famous artist, paint a mural in the Sala Regia (Throne Room) of the Vatican, commemorating the slaughter. Vasari did a particularly good job of depicting the bloody destruction of so many loyal Frenchmen, who were guilty only of believing in freedom of conscience.

What does the Vatican think of this historic event that the Roman Church had such big a part in? Decide for yourself. Vasari's mural still hangs within sight of the Pope's throne. It is a symbol of triumph of Roman Catholicism over all other faiths. Their world view is still this, as evidenced by Pope Benedict's recent statement.

How did Pope Gregori XIII view himself? His "heraldic" symbol was the great **Red Dragon of Satan.** (You can read about the Red Dragon in the Book of Revelation, chapter 12.)

Incidentally, prior to becoming Pope, Gregori was a delegate to the Council of Trent. Further, he was guilty of scandalous conduct, including fathering an illegitimate son. Such conduct was common for the leadership of the Roman Church at the time.

Altar Footstool

Remember the previous quote: "A Pope is the absolute judge of his own actions, in all circumstances." Consider the following:

> In the ceremony called the Adoration of the Pope, which takes place almost immediately after his election, He is placed in a chair on the altar of the Sistine Chapel, and there receives the homage of the cardinals; this ceremony is again repeated on the high altar of St. Peter. But why should the altar be made his foot stool? The altar, the beauty of holiness, the throne of the victim-lamb, the mercy seat of the Temple of Christianity; why should the altar be converted into the footstool of a mortal? Why, indeed, but as a fulfillment of the apostolic prediction, "He as God sitteth in the Temple of God, showing himself that he is God" (*A Text Book on Popery, a brief history of the Council of Trent*, J.D. Cramp; Page 374).

Again, the title of this ritual is "the **Adoration** of the Pope." One primary meaning of the word **adoration** is worship. The actions taken during this ritual clearly demonstrate that the Pope is "worshipped." In ancient Roman paganism, kings and emperors were frequently elevated to "god" status and then worshipped. It is easily understood that the ritual described above has, at its intent, that purpose for the Pope. Here the Roman church has copied ancient Roman paganism.

Kidnapping of Edgardo Mortara

Escape From Paganism

I magine that you are a parent of a six-month-old baby. Ever had one? What are your memories? What were your fears for the little one?

The Mortara family of Bologna, Italy, had such a baby, his name was Edgardo. The Mortara's were Jews. The Mortara family had seven other children. To help Mom care for them all, and keep house, the Mortara's hired a servant girl.

The girl was an ardent Roman Catholic and feared for Edgardo, that if he should die, he would go to hell because he was not baptized. So, she baptized Edgardo and told the Catholic authorities about it. A report was brought to Pope Pius IX. Since Bologna was a Papal "state," he ordered the office of Inquisition to seize the boy, which they did on June 23, 1858.

Pope Pius IX refused to return the boy to the parents, in spite of the worldwide public outrage it created. Edgardo was raised in a convent and went on to be ordained a priest. He was never reunited with his parents. Edgardo died in 1940.

How does the Roman Church view this action today? You can only judge by their actions on behalf of the chief orchestrator of the incident, Pope Pius IX. In the year 2000, Pius IX was "beatified" by Pope John Paul II.

What is beatification?

A stage in the process of canonization, involving a declaration by the Pope that the candidate is enjoying heavenly bliss and can be venerated.

Canonization is the declaration that the individual is a saint. So, being "beatified," Pius IX is one step away from being declared a saint by the Roman Church. It is interesting to note, also, that having been beatified; he is now to be **"venerated."** Veneration means to worship – like we worship God. In this case we would be worshipping a kidnapper.

Note: According to *The Oxford American Desk Dictionary & Thesaurus,* to venerate means to honor, esteem, **to worship.**

It can only be that the Roman Church still sanctions the kidnapping of the Mortara baby, since the architect of the scheme has now been beatified and is worshipped (venerated) as a god.

Is the Pope the Supreme Ruler of the World?

What we have seen so far of the Roman Catholic world view is how their belief in the primacy of the Pope can work itself out. It is clear that their view of the primacy of the Pope means that He is, rightfully, the Supreme Ruler of the world.

We have seen that the Roman Church considers itself to be **the only church** that has salvation available to its members. One cannot be saved outside of the Roman Church. We have seen this exclusivity expressed in their canon law and we have seen this exclusivity and uniqueness expressed as persecution of those who believe differently than the Roman Church. We have seen that the persecution previously cited is still celebrated as proper action by them.

How are we to understand the Roman Church reaching out to Lutherans, Anglicans, the Reformed and Evangelicals, trying to bring everyone together ecumenically? Let's look at what they have done and what has to be their "infallible" view of these efforts.

> The origin of the Pontifical Council for Promoting Christian Unity is closely linked with the Second Vatican Council. It was Pope John XXIII's desire that the involvement of the Catholic Church in the contemporary ecumenical movement be one of the Council's chief concerns. Thus, on 5 June 1960, he established a "Secretariat for Promoting Christian Unity" as one of the preparatory commissions for the Council, and appointed Cardinal Augustin Bea as its first President. This was the first time that the Roman Church had set up an office to deal uniquely with ecumenical affairs.
>
> At present, the PCPCU is engaged in an international theological dialogue with each of the following Churches and World Communions:
>
> The Orthodox Church
>
> The Coptic Orthodox Church
>
> The Malankara Churches

The Anglican Communion

The Lutheran World Federation

The World Alliance of Reformed Churches

The World Methodist Council

The Baptist World Alliance

The Christian Church (Disciples of Christ)

Some Pentecostal groups.

The Council also seeks to promote meetings with Evangelicals (www.vatican.va/roman_curia/pontifical_councils/chrstuni/documents/rc_pc_chrstuni_pro_20051996_chrstuni_pro_en.html.)

What are they doing? Look again at their history and Canon law. Remember, they claim infallibility. They cannot make mistakes. Their historical acts have been embraced by their recent actions. Their canon law remains and will continue. Specifically what is the concern?

Jon Hus was under a safe conduct pass to debate issues at the Council of Constance. He was burned at the stake, because the Roman Church stated that it could not keep its word to heretics. "An oath sworn against the good of the Church does not bind; because that is not an oath, but a perjury rather, which is taken against the Church's interests (see Decreti Gregorii, lib. Ii, tit. xxiv., cap. xxvii).

Since the determination of "the good of the Church" can come at anytime it moves them to determine it, one is foolish to trust it. Who knows whether what is thought "good" today, will continue to be thought "good" tomorrow? This was the conclusion that Luther and others, invited to debate at the Council of Trent came to. There is nothing in Rome's word to trust, knowing the history of Jon Hus and the relevant Canon law.

Notice also, their disdain for Protestants: "It is wicked to allow Protestants equal rights with Roman Catholics." With this viewpoint, how can any agreement with Protestants be considered "good" for the Roman Church? It would seem that any agreement they make with Protestants would be a lie, or a "perjury" against the church, as they put it.

Finally, there is the primacy of the Pope that comes into play:

> A Pope is the absolute judge of his own actions, in all circumstances, and that he could annul the promises he had previously made (*Cormenin's History*, 2, 111).
>
> Innocent III laid down the proud maxim that out of the fullness of his power, he might lawfully dispense with the law (*Europe During the Middle Ages* by Hallam, p. 373).

There are some amazing inferences a rational person has to draw. Trusting the word of the Roman Church does not seem to be a rational act.

Summary

The Roman Catholic Church has held these world views for at least 1,700 years. It has not changed and it will not change, of itself or man.

In light of the long history of the Roman Church, here are some quotes of rather recent vintage. Remember, we are talking about the infallible church, it claims not to make mistakes and this being the case, the course of the church has not changed. Quotes are from *Roman Catholicism,* by Lorraine Boettner.

> Fr. Marianus de Luca, S. J., Professor of Canon Law at the Gregorian University in Rome, said in his Institution of Public Ecclesiastical Law, with a personal commendation from Pope Leo XIII, in 1901:
>
> The Catholic Church has the right and duty to kill heretics because it is by fire and sword that heresy can be extirpated. Mass excommunication is derided by heretics. If they are imprisoned or exiled they corrupt others. The only recourse is to put them to death. Repentance cannot be allowed to save them, just as repentance is not allowed to save civil criminals; for the highest good of the church is the duty of the faith, and this cannot be preserved unless heretics are put to death.
>
> The official newspaper of the large Roman Catholic diocese of Brooklyn, New York, *The Tablet,* in its issue of November 5, 1938, declared:
>
> Heresy is an awful crime ... and those who start a heresy are more guilty than they who are traitors to the civil government. If the State has the right to punish treason with death, the principle is the same which concedes to the spiritual authority the power of capital punishment over the archtraitor to truth and Divine revelation....A perfect society has the right to its existence ... and the power of capital punishment is acknowledged for a perfect society. Now ... the Roman Catholic Church is a perfect society, and as such has the right and power to take means to safeguard its existence.
>
> In the following words by a present day (1960s) American Roman Catholic theologian, Francis J. Connell, with imprimatur by Cardinal Spellman, even the right of existence is denied to other churches:
>
> The Catholic Church is the only organization authorized by God to teach religious truth and to conduct public religious worship.

Consequently, they [Roman Catholics] hold that any creed which differs from that of the Catholic Church is erroneous, and that any religious organization which is separated from the Catholic Church lacks the approval and the authorization of God. The very existence of any other church is opposed to the command of Christ, that all men should join His one church. From this it follows that, as far as God's law is concerned, **no one has a real right to accept any religion save the Catholic Church**" (*Freedom of Worship, the Catholic Position*).

Have we not seen the last one reaffirmed by the current pope? Should they regain the political power they had in the 17th century and before, would we not see the first two restored as a matter of practice?

God's World View

God Has Spoken!

Who is this God who has spoken? What has He said? Where do I learn what He has said?

To quote an old adage: "out of sight, is out of mind," but is God truly out of sight? Humanity generally ignores God and His Words are viewed with disbelief. But disbelief will only get us in trouble. God not only thinks He is boss, but is!

What is your concept of "God-ness." My computer has one. Just now, when I typed "Godness," spell-checker changed the word to "goodness." That is good, because God's goodness is great. There is no "badness" or evil in God, but how do we know this?

Man is capable of defining or understanding anything that his "senses" can reveal to him. We humans need to see, taste, touch, smell, or hear something to comprehend it. We are in darkness regarding anything that exists beyond our natural human abilities to discern.

Man has one other "sense," however, which makes some think we are reaching beyond our basic senses for understanding. This other "sense" is our imagination or "make believe." In and of our own ability, we cannot see, touch, smell, hear or taste anything beyond our real time or physical world.

What does this have to do with God speaking? If there is a God, and if this God wants us to know anything about Him, then God must reveal Himself to man. Why? God must reveal Himself to man because if He is God, He has to exist above the order, or "laws" of the physical world, which He created. We can infer from the order of the physical realm that God must exist, that He must be great and all powerful, but little else is discernable.

God's existence is revealed by His creation, our physical realm; He is beyond our sensible ability to fully comprehend by our senses, but He has spoken. He has spoken so He could reveal His purpose for creation and His purpose for man. His purpose is His world view.

God Is Boss

He Is the Boss as He Is the Creator!

> In the beginning was the Word, and the Word was with God, and the Word was God. The same was in the beginning with God. All things were made through him; and without him was not anything made that hath been made. In him was life; and the life was the light of men. And the light shineth in the darkness; and the darkness apprehended it not (John 1:1-5 ASV).

Much information is provided in this short passage. First, we learn there was a "beginning." A beginning is the point at which something was not, and then is.

What is it that was not, that now is? This passage states "all things." The beginning of **all things.** Man cannot "sense" the meaning of anything prior to the beginning as there were no "things" to sense. No physical or sensible existence "was" prior to **all** things coming into existence through Him.

"All things" refers to the "natural" order of things, which we see around us. In the beginning the Word was; God was, and the Word was God. In the beginning, God, and God the Word were already in existence. All things that came into existence came through the Word. Think of what comprises the "all things:" time, space, the elements, the planets, molecules, animals, plant life, human kind, all things. All things came into being through God the Word, as directed by God, the Father.

> In the beginning God created the heavens and the earth. And the earth was waste and void; and darkness was upon the face of the deep: and the Spirit of God moved upon the face of the waters (Genesis 1:1-2 ASV).

In English, we miss a point here. The word "God," above, is *Elohim* in Hebrew. *El* is the name for God in the singular. The word *Elohim* is the plural form for God. God in His plural form is being discussed in these verses. We have already seen in John 1 that **the Word is God** and that **He was with God.** In Genesis 1:2, the Spirit of God is revealed. In the very first verses of the

Bible, we are introduced to the one God, in three persons: God, the Word and Holy Spirit.

GOD HAS SPOKEN

God has spoken through His Word. In Genesis 1:3, 6, 9, 11, 14, 20, 24, and 25, we see that "God said." Each time He spoke, some part of creation sprang into existence. At this point, God had spoken all creation into being. All of the "all things" that were to be created, have been created. Nothing new will be created. What message to man was created through God's act of speaking creation into existence?

> For the invisible things of him since the creation of the world are clearly seen, being perceived through the things that are made, *even* his everlasting power and divinity; that they may be without excuse (Romans 1:20 ASV).

From creation and from what God through His Word has done, we can and should know about Him, His power, divinity, and that He created everything. Do we? No! Many have embraced make-believe science in the form of evolution to explain how we are, what we are, and how creation is what it is. Remember that we can only discern what our senses reveal to us. To reach out and explain the "beginning of things" (a time before which there was nothing) is beyond our ability to sense. There are two basic physical laws, the laws of conservation and decay, which state, implicitly, that there was a beginning – a time before which there was nothing in the natural order of things.

GOD HAS SPOKEN

So here we are as it says in Romans 1:20, "without excuse."

What else do we know about creation at this point? The Apostle Paul wrote this to explain our existence.

> The God that made the world and all things therein, he, being Lord of heaven and earth, dwelleth not in temples made with hands; neither is he served by men's hands, as though he needed anything, seeing he himself giveth to all life, and breath, and all things; and he made of one every nation of men to dwell on all the face of the earth, having determined *their* appointed seasons, and the bounds of their habitation; that they should seek God, if haply they might feel after him and find

him, though he is not far from each one of us: for in him we live, and move, and have our being; as certain even of your own poets have said (Acts 17:24-28 ASV).

GOD HAS SPOKEN

Consider another way our Creator has revealed Himself: "God ... spoke long ago to the fathers in the prophets in many portions and in many ways" (Hebrews 1:1). This verse tells us that God spoke to the ancients through His prophets. From this "speaking" we received the body of revelation we call the Old Testament. This body of writings is referred to as "The Law and the Prophets" in the New Testament.

Here we are told how God verbally revealed Himself to man in many ways. Numerous Old Testament revelations have to do with the coming of Christ. God's revelation was at times accomplished by the Spirit of Christ in the prophets.

> Concerning which salvation the prophets sought and searched diligently, who prophesied of the grace that *should come* unto you: searching what *time* or what manner of time the Spirit of Christ which was in them did point unto, when it testified beforehand the sufferings of Christ, and the glories that should follow them (1 Peter 1:10, 11 ASV).

Christ told them He was coming. This was God the Son, the pre-incarnate Christ, testifying to the prophets of His coming, hundreds or even thousands of years prior to His coming to earth as a man.

Noah preached Christ's words to the people of the earth for 120 years. These people were destroyed by the flood and are now in prison, awaiting the second death.

> Because Christ also suffered for sins once, the righteous for the unrighteous, that he might bring us to God; being put to death in the flesh, but made alive in the spirit; in which also he went and preached unto the spirits in prison (1 Peter 3:18, 19 ASV).

The Word of the Lord was used in revealing God to man: "After these things the Word of the Lord came to Abram" (Genesis 15:1). The **Word** of the Lord is identified as God in John 1. Later in that chapter, we are told that the Word took on flesh and dwelt among us. This Word is none other than Jesus

Christ. "The words of Jeremiah the son of Hilkiah, of the priests who were in Anathoth in the land of Benjamin, to whom the word of the Lord came" (Jeremiah 1:1, 2).

God also used visions and dreams to reveal Himself. "God spoke to Israel in visions" (Genesis 46:2) and He said, "Hear now my words: If there is a prophet among you, I, the Lord, shall make Myself known to him in a vision. I shall speak with him in a dream" (Numbers 12:6).

The Angel of the Lord is none other than the pre-incarnate Christ. Pre-incarnate means "before He took on flesh." The pre-incarnate Christ is Jesus before He became man.

> And the angel of Jehovah called unto him out of heaven, and said, Abraham, Abraham. And he said, Here I am (Genesis 22:11 ASV).
>
> And the angel of Jehovah appeared unto him in a flame of fire out of the midst of a bush: and he looked, and, behold, the bush burned with fire, and the bush was not consumed (Exodus 3:2 ASV).

The Bible shows that God spoke to the fathers in various ways through the prophets. The Bible also makes this claim: "The grass withers, the flower fades, but the word of our God stands forever" (Isaiah 40:8).

God is serious about what He says and declared, "I am the Alpha and the Omega," says the Lord God, "who is and who was and who is to come, the Almighty" (Revelation 1:8). He is the alpha and omega–the beginning and end. He made it all, knows it all from eternity past to eternity future, and makes no mistakes. It behooves all men to pay attention.

The Alpha and Omega

T**he Alpha and Omega** are the first and last letters in the Greek alphabet. God the Son is speaking in Revelation 1:8. Jesus Christ claims to be the Alpha and Omega, existing before the beginning and will exist after the ending. The Apostle John wrote:

> In the beginning was the Word, and the Word was with God, and the Word was God. The same was in the beginning with God . . . And the Word became flesh, and dwelt among us (and we beheld his glory, glory as of the only begotten from the Father), full of grace and truth (John 1:1-2, 14 ASV).

This verse tells us that the Word became flesh. The Word became man—like us. The balance of the chapter makes it clear that Christ is the Word. Christ has a key role in revealing God to man. "For the Law was given through Moses; grace and truth were realized through Jesus Christ" (v. 17) and "No one has seen God at any time; the only begotten God who is in the bosom of the Father, He has explained Him" (v. 18). Christ has explained God to mankind.

Jesus Christ is the Word, which means Jesus Christ, God, existed in eternity past. Jesus Christ, the Word came down from heaven to earth to become a man. He did not give up being God, yet He also became man. He was and is fully man and fully God. The natures were not mixed or confounded.

GOD SPOKE TO US IN HIS SON.

> God, having of old time spoken unto the fathers in the prophets by divers portions and in divers manners, hath at the end of these days spoken unto us in his Son, whom he appointed heir of all things, through whom also he made the worlds; who being the effulgence of his glory, and the very image of his substance, and upholding all things by the word of his power, when he had made purification of sins, sat down on the right hand of the Majesty on high (Hebrews 1:1-3 ASV).

Jesus Christ is upholding **all things** by the "word of His power." These are the same "all things" that were created in the beginning. Imagine the power, the knowledge, and the infinite capacity of our God.

God Has Spoken through the Apostles

After Christ's ascension to the right hand of the Father in heaven, God continued to speak through the apostles. These writers were under the inspiration of the Holy Spirit and the New Testament is the result of this revelation.

> He that loveth me not keepeth not my words: and the word which ye hear is not mine, but the Father's who sent me. These things have I spoken unto you, while yet abiding with you. But the Comforter, even the Holy Spirit, whom the Father will send in my name, he shall teach you all things, and bring to your remembrance all that I said unto you (John 14:24-26 ASV).

Who is an apostle?

> The former treatise I made, O Theophilus, concerning all that Jesus began both to do and to teach, until the day in which he was received up, after that he had given commandment through the Holy Spirit unto the apostles whom he had chosen: to whom he also showed himself alive after his passion by many proofs, appearing unto them by the space of forty days, and speaking the things concerning the kingdom of God: and, being assembled together with them, he charged them not to depart from Jerusalem, but to wait for the promise of the Father, which, said he, ye heard from me: for John indeed baptized with water; but ye shall be baptized in the Holy Spirit not many days hence (Acts 1:2, 3 ASV) (Also see 1 Cor. 9:1; Acts 1:21, 22.)

Luke wrote that the apostles were chosen by Christ and that they had seen the Lord after His resurrection. One had to satisfy these requirements to be an apostle. There are no apostles today. There have been none since the original apostles died off.

God's Word Is Complete

A major role of the apostles, the recording of Scripture- the New Testament, is complete. God's revelation of Himself is complete for this time period. There is no such thing as "apostolic succession."

Christ gives this dire warning:

> I testify unto every man that heareth the words of the prophecy of this book, if any man shall add unto them, God shall add unto him the plagues which are written in this book: and if any man shall take away from the words of the book of this prophecy, God shall take away his part from the tree of life, and out of the holy city, which are written in this book (Revelation 22:18- 19 ASV).

God's revelation of Himself is complete for now, and we are promised blessings if we heed the Word we have been given: "And behold, I am coming quickly. Blessed is he who heeds the words of the prophecy of this book" (Revelation 22:7). The all-mighty, all-knowing, eternal, good, and glorious, creator God has spoken! His words are the first and last authority for faith and practice.

GOD HAS SPOKEN!

If any commentator, teacher, church leader, denominational or church law, advances the idea that the church fathers, tradition, or apostolic authority is equal or superior to God's word - **flee!** It is the anti-christ at work. Here is what Jesus Christ says about keeping His words, "He who does not love Me does not keep My words; and the word which you hear is not Mine, but the Father's who sent Me" (John 14:23).

All of us need to copy the Bereans.

> Now these were more noble than those in Thessalonica, in that they received the word with all readiness of the mind, examining the Scriptures daily, whether these things were so (Acts 17:11 ASV).

God has ordained that:
> Every scripture inspired of God *is* also profitable for teaching, for reproof, for correction, for instruction which is in righteousness. That the man of God may be complete, furnished completely unto every good work (2 Timothy 3:16, 17 ASV).

It is amazing that God has patiently revealed His will to man over the past several thousand years. He takes that revelation seriously:

> I have overthrown *cities* among you, as when God overthrew Sodom and Gomorrah, and ye were as a brand plucked out of the burning: yet have ye not returned unto me, saith Jehovah.
>
> Therefore thus will I do unto thee, O Israel; *and* because I will do this unto thee, prepare to meet thy God, O Israel. For, lo, he that formeth the mountains, and createth the wind, and declareth unto man what is his thought; that maketh the morning darkness, and treadeth upon the high places of the Earth—Jehovah, the God of hosts, is his name (Amos 4:11-13 ASV).

Biblical Proof That The Roman Church Is Pagan

What is "paganism?"

> **Paganism** (from Latin paganus, meaning "country dweller, rustic") is a word used to refer to various religions and religious beliefs from across the world. It is a term which, from a Western perspective, has modern connotations of spiritualist, animistic or shamanic practices or beliefs of any folk religion, and of historical and contemporary polytheistic religions in particular.
>
> The term "pagan" is a Christian adaptation of the term "gentile" of Judaism. (http://en.wikipedia.org/wiki/Paganism)

The word Gentile is the equivalent of Pagan. Here is what Jesus had to say about the prayers of the Gentiles or Pagans:

> And in praying use not vain repetitions, as the Gentiles do: for they think that they shall be heard for their much speaking. Be not therefore like unto them: for your Father knoweth what things ye have need of, before ye ask him (Matthew 6:7-8 ASV).

Christ criticized vain, repetitious prayers, stating that it was something the Gentiles did. Who were the Gentiles? They were anyone outside of Israel. But there was a specific branch of the Gentiles that He referred to. Who was it? Well, they are Pagans for sure, read on:

> And as Jesus was going up to Jerusalem, he took the twelve disciples apart, and on the way he said unto them, Behold, we go up to Jerusalem; and the Son of man shall be delivered unto the chief priests and scribes; and they shall condemn him to death, and shall deliver him unto the Gentiles to mock, and to scourge, and to crucify: and the third day he shall be raised up (Matthew 20:17-19 ASV).
>
> And they shall fall by the edge of the sword, and shall be led captive into all the nations: and Jerusalem shall be trodden down of the Gentiles, until the times of the Gentiles be fulfilled (Luke 21:24 ASV).

Here are two more hints about who they were. This branch of the Gentiles mocked, scourged and crucified Christ. Further, they treaded down Jerusalem.

> And they bound him, and led him away, and delivered him up to Pilate the governor (Matthew 27:2 ASV).

> So when Pilate saw that he prevailed nothing, but rather that a tumult was arising, he took water, and washed his hands before the multitude, saying, I am innocent of the blood of this righteous man; see ye to it. And all the people answered and said, His blood be on us, and on our children. Then released he unto them Barabbas; but Jesus he scourged and delivered to be crucified (Matthew 27:24-26 ASV).

Rome was the branch of the Gentiles (Pagans) that scourged, mocked and crucified Christ. They, like all Gentiles, used vain repetitious prayers in their Pagan religious rituals. So, what has this to do with the Roman Church? It is the Christian Church that replaced paganism, right?

Wrong, paganism replaced Christianity, putting on a full head of steam about the time of Emperor Constantine's "conversion."

As more proof of the conversion of Christianity to Paganism, in the Roman Church, consider the books named Missal, and Ritual.

MISSAL:

> (Latin *Missale* from *Missa, Mass*), the book which contains the **prayers** said by the priest at the alter as well as all that is officially read or sung in connection with the offering of the holy Sacrifice of the Mass through the ecclesiastical year (www.newadvent.org).

RITUAL:

> The Ritual *(Rituale Romanum)* is one of the official books of the Roman Rite. It contains all the services performed by a priest that are not in the Missal and Breviary and has also, for convenience, some that are in those books. It is the latest and still the least uniform book of our rite (www.newadvent.org).

Christ's reference to Gentiles and vain repetitious prayer encompassed all Gentiles. However, He stated this in a way that reveals that His disciples would have firsthand knowledge of how the Gentiles pray. That would mean that they had probably witnessed some religious exercises by the Gentiles. Since it was

Gentile (Pagan) Rome that scourged, mocked and crucified Christ and since it was Rome that really ruled Palestine, one must understand that the visible witness of the truth of Christ's statement was primarily Pagan Rome.

As you see in the books *Missal* and *Ritual*, the prayers and "antics" (choreography) of the priests are preprinted and said (and performed) over and over and over again. This is in direct violation of Christ's instructions. It is a Pagan practice. These books with their prayers and choreographies are rebellion against the living God. Remember Adam? He did not believe God's Word and because of this, caused us a lot of trouble.

Rome merely adopted a page from the Pagan book of ritual. But why not, the Roman Church is Pagan. As you will see they are polytheistic also; they have a belief in many gods.

The rest of this book will provide you with more substance that proves the Roman Church is Pagan.

Is Man God?

Jack and Jill,
Went up the hill,
To fetch a pail of water.
Jack fell down,
And broke his crown,
And Jill came tumbling after.

Jack and Jill,
Went up the hill,
To fetch a pail of water.
Jack fell down ...

But I repeat myself, why?

Have you ever heard a recording lapse into endless loop? Something goes wrong with the mechanism and it plays the same thing over and over. The old wax based records could do that. They could get scratched and when the pickup needle got to that point, it would follow the scratch back to the beginning point and play it again.

The Roman Catholic teaching about salvation is that way. According to them, you can never be sure of your salvation. You hit a "scratch" in life—sin—and lose your salvation. You have to get saved over and over again and then pay for your sins by spending an interminable amount of time in a hot spot called Purgatory. This cycle of salvation, sin, salvation will become apparent as we study some of the sacraments individually.

In the sacraments we will see how the Roman Church teaches that one can achieve salvation. You achieve things through work. This achievement raises the questions: Can Roman Catholics be "saved," believing what they believe? Can man be saved by works? Can anyone be saved in the Roman Catholic system? Well, maybe not, as what is achieved is only temporary at best.

God established the way of salvation. As recorded in John 14:6, Jesus Christ said, "I am the Way, the Truth, and the Life; no one comes to the Father except by me." As we will see there are multiple passages in the Gospel of John that show salvation is by faith. Other passages throughout the New Testament reveal that all man can "achieve" by his works is damnation!

Yet, the Roman Catholic Church has established a mechanical, or magical, means of salvation that rejects Christ's statement recorded in John 14:6. A Roman Catholic ritual entitled *The Adoration of the Pope* involves raising the pope high enough so that the "altar of Christ" becomes his footstool. In short, the Pope replaces God, thereby posing the question: Is man God?

In a recent book, two priests attempt to answer the question: Are Catholics Christian?

> Yes, Catholics are Christian, as are Protestants and Eastern Orthodox Christians. A Christian is someone who **professes** the belief that Jesus Christ is the Son of God and that He is the Savior of mankind ... (*The Catholicism Answer Book,* Rev. John Trigilio, Jr., PHD, THD, & Rev. Kenneth Brighenti, PHD).

The answer above appears to be an expression of faith in Jesus Christ, alone, as Savior. But it cannot be, for if it were, the writers would be held as heretics and damned if tried under canon law. Here is what the Roman Catechism says:

> If anyone says that by faith alone the impious is justified ... let him be anathema.

Note the word "professes." It allows the answer they have stated, but still enables them "wiggle room" to get back to sacramental works.

What is my objection here about the word profess? Notice that they state "profess to believe." Why profess to believe? Why not just say that "we believe." Why "profess to believe?" Or simply we profess Christ as the Son of God and the Savior of mankind? ***Webster's New World Dictionary*** gives this description for the word profess: "to claim to have (some feeling, an interest, knowledge, etc.) **often** connoting insincerity or pretense."

Sure, a profession could be a sincere and real expression of one's belief. However, a profession can be pretended and in this case, such is the fact. Remember, the Bible states that we must believe in Christ as our Savior and Lord alone, to be saved. The Roman Church requires belief in many things and people.

In our examination of the sacraments, we will see how Roman belief is really in the mechanical or magical aspects of the sacraments. The Roman Church does not believe in the divine actions of God the Father, God the Son and God the Spirit in changing man from the first Adam to the second Adam and thereby becoming an eternal child of God.

The quote from the previously cited book was rank double talk. It is opposite of what the final definer of truth for the Roman Catholic says about this. Who is the final definer? According to Roman Canon law, it is the Pope. Pope Benedict recently stated that no one can be saved outside of the mother Church, which is the Roman Catholic Church. If you cannot be saved outside of the Roman Catholic Church, you are not a Christian, so said the Pope, while he was still Cardinal Ratzinger. This was restated in July, 2007 as Pope. By the way, to be a Christian you have to be "saved," which means born again.

The Vatican's current position was affirmed by the Council of Trent when they established their catechism. Pope Benedict's words are the historic position of Roman Catholicism. It was reaffirmed by Vatican II. According to these resources, to be a Christian, you must be a member of the Roman Church and participate in the sacraments. If you **merely trust in your "profession" of Christ**, you are damned.

The purpose of this book is to show the means of salvation. For the Roman Church, some of those supposed means are the sacraments we are examining now. Does the Pope or the Vatican have a clue? Is everyone else damned or are those who believe Roman Catholic Theology damned? The Pope has put this issue on either or terms. Well, not really, it is God who has spoken; He has dictated the terms.

One more comment about this term "profess." The demons also believe, and tremble (see James 2:19). Belief has to be according to the requirements laid down in Scripture. Further, belief cannot be mixed with the works of man or mechanical, magical, means of salvation. Belief, or faith, is in Christ alone, His **finished** work and Lordship. Belief is this: "for by grace you are saved, through faith, and that not of yourself, it is a gift of God" (Ephesians 2:8).

Remember, the Roman Church professes to change one from the **outside in** with the sacraments. God says this is false because we need to be changed from the **inside out** and only He can do this. Consider Jesus' own words from the Book of Luke:

> Now as he spake, a Pharisee asketh him to dine with him: and he went in, and sat down to meat. And when the Pharisee saw it, he marveled that he had not first bathed himself before dinner. And the Lord said unto him, now ye the Pharisees cleanse the outside of the cup and of the platter; but your inward part is full of extortion and wickedness. Ye foolish ones, did not he that made the outside make the inside also? (Luke 11:37-40 ASV).

God did make both the inside and the outside. God is the only one that can clean up the inside. He does this through our faith and spiritual re-birth, not through sacraments. The process is called sanctification and it is accomplished by the indwelling Holy Spirit.

The Clay's War with The Potter

Escape From Paganism

Back when I was young—say late 30s, early 40s, a typical birthday, Christmas, or just a play day gift, would be colored molding clay. It was a great imagination builder. A child could make just about anything that could be conjured up with this clay.

But did you hear about the child, who, early one morning, unable to sleep, crept down the dark stairs to the playroom? It was unusually dark as he entered the playroom.

"What's happening?" he exclaimed, as something moist and firm grabbed him and wrestled him to the wall. To keep him quiet, this "thing" stuffed some of its substance into the child's mouth, stopping the child from crying out in alarm. For the next hour this "thing" forced the child in all kinds of funny positions. The child, of course, was terrified.

Day began to break and the child could see that the "thing" was his clay. His clay was doing to him what he did to it in his play. The clay had taken charge of the master. Well, his parents would never believe him—would you?

What about our relationship with God? He is the potter, we are the clay. Can we control God?

> But now, O Jehovah, thou art our Father; we are the clay, and thou our potter; and we all are the work of thy hand (Isaiah 64:8 ASV).

> Ye turn things upside down! Shall the potter be esteemed as clay; that the thing made should say of him that made it, He made me not; or the thing formed say of him that formed it, He hath no understanding? (Isaiah 29:16 ASV).

> Who hath declared it from the beginning, that we may know? and beforetime, that we may say, *He is* right? yea, there is none that declareth, yea, there is none that showeth, yea, there is none that heareth your words (Isaiah 41:26 ASV).

God has a plan for His creation. He has clearly told us this plan in His owner's manual, the Bible. But from Adam on, we have all rejected it.

God is the Potter; remember how He made Adam? The very name Adam describes how God created him. Adam means earth. Our original ancestor was from the earth, as are all of us since Adam. We are the clay, the creation of God the Father. God is Spirit. God is of Himself. He is the one in which all creation exists.

Man, in Adam, is at enmity with God (see Romans 8:7) and pays scant attention to what He says. Man in Adam thinks he knows more about how to be righteous than God. Adam and Eve's first son, Cain, demonstrated this by his offerings. When his offering was rejected, he murdered his brother Abel (see Genesis 4:1-8). All men, from the first Adam on down, have rejected the words of the Potter.

This has been the cause of natural man's enslavement to sin and death. God put a fresh lump onto the potter's wheel and made a new creation, the second Adam, the body of Jesus Christ.

> Wherefore when he cometh into the world, he saith, "Sacrifice and offering thou wouldest not, But a body didst thou prepare for me" (Hebrews 10:5 ASV).
>
> Since then the children are sharers in flesh and blood, he also himself in like manner partook of the same; that through death he might bring to nought him that had the power of death, that is, the devil (Hebrews 2:14 ASV).

God sent His Son to be born a man from the womb of the virgin, Mary. God, the Son, took on a body, humanity, created by God the Father. This body was a "new lump" in that it was conceived of the Holy Spirit in the womb of the "woman" (remember the Seed of the Woman from Genesis 3) and was free of the sin nature (the contamination of original sin). Jesus is the second Adam, the first born of a new race of mankind. Christ is and was obedient to His Father's plan. The result is that many regenerated into the race of the second Adam, His body, the Church, and the coming Kingdom.

As we will see later, this leads to the Mystery, the church, which encompasses people from all nations. Then we are led to a great controversy. The controversy of the Roman Church, which claims to be Christian, but at the same time is telling the Potter that they know more than He knows about how to qualify for eternal life.

This "church" is of the earth, a part of the Potter's creation. Can this church know more than He? Do they really have the ability to tell the Potter what is right and what is wrong? We are going to examine concepts such as Vicar of Christ, Sacraments, Purgatory, Ritual, Relics, Images, Saints, and the Virgin Mary.

Our guide for truth will be the Word of God, the Bible. We should have our Bible at our side as we study this. Remember, the consequences of allowing ourselves to be deceived are horrific!

Our primary guide for information on the sacraments and other subjects will be the Catholic Catechism of the Council of Trent, and the history of the Council of Trent.

Subsequent to Vatican II, does Trent still apply? Yes. According to an official Catholic Church document:

> The sacred council accepts loyally the venerable faith of our ancestors in the living communion which exists between us and our brothers who are in the glory of heaven or who are yet being purified after their death; and it proposes again the decrees of the Second Council of Nicea, of the Council of Florence, and of the Council of Trent (Vatican Council II, Vol. 1, *The Conciliar and Post Conciliar Documents,* p.412).

The rest will be from other historical sources.

Vicar of Christ

One title of the Pope in Rome is Vicar of Christ. Vicar means "substitute." The Pope is vaunted as the substitute for Christ on earth, and whatever he says about the rule of "Faith" is what the Roman Church must believe.

> The infallible judgment of the Church is pronounced through him. This infallibility is not personal, but official. As a man, the Pope may be immoral, heretical, or infidel; as Pope, when speaking ex cathedra, he is the organ of the Holy Spirit (*Systematic Theology*, Volume 1, Page 112, Charles Hodge).

We will see that the active minute-by-minute head of the Church is Jesus Christ and that as the Cornerstone, He runs His Church through the Living Stones that make up the Church. These Living Stones are individual believers gifted for the service of building up and helping to nourish the body (the Church). Christ does not have a substitute, need a substitute, or want a substitute. Therefore, the Roman Catholic Doctrine that the Pope is Vicar of Christ is false. Further, we will see that the Church that Christ heads is local, it is not denominational, or political.

This brings us to another title for the Pope. That title is "Anti-Christ." Since he pretends to be "in place" (Vicar) of Christ, the successor to something that needs not to be succeeded, and therefore is operating in opposition to the will of God and Christ, the term Anti Christ fits.

> He saith unto them, "But who say ye that I am?" And Simon Peter answered and said, "Thou art the Christ, the Son of the living God." And Jesus answered and said unto him, "Blessed art thou, Simon Bar-Jonah: for flesh and blood hath not revealed it unto thee, but my Father who is in heaven. And I also say unto thee, that thou art Peter, and upon this rock I will build my church; and the gates of Hades shall not prevail against it. I will give unto thee the keys of the kingdom of heaven: and whatsoever thou shalt bind on earth shall be bound in heaven; and whatsoever thou shalt loose on earth shall be loosed in heaven" (Matthew 16:15-19 ASV).

In his response to the Lord's question, "Who do you say that I am?" Peter confesses Christ.

In many languages, nouns have a "gender." Some nouns are masculine, some are feminine, and some are neutral. The Greek language (the language the New Testament was written in) is one of these. The word "confession" is not used in the preceding verse, but it does describe what Peter said. "You are the Christ, the Son of the living God." The word "confess" (Greek = homologia) is of the feminine gender.

This will be examined in detail later. But let it be said that this is the verse that the Roman Church bases its doctrine of apostolic succession upon as well as their basis that Peter was the first pope. As we shall see, they have twisted the Scriptures. There is no such thing as apostolic succession. Since this is so, the claim by Rome of possessing the Keys to Heaven is also without foundation.

The person who is called Vicar of Christ is an enemy, not a representative, of Jesus Christ. There was even a Pope that agreed with this position. Pope Gregory, the Great, stated in 595, "whosoever should declare himself "universal bishop" would deserve to be regarded as the forerunner of antichrist" (*History of the Council of Trent*, page 71, J.D. Cramp).

Further proof of this can be deduced from Jesus' words in Matthew 7:16 & 20: "you shall know them by their fruit." If apostolic succession was a real situation, that is, if all the Popes were successors of the apostles, you would expect a godly line of men to have led the Roman Church. That would mean a godly line without a break. Instead, you find a line of ordinary men subject to sin and regularly succumbing to it. Here are some glaringly grotesque examples:

- Liberius, 357 AD, was an Arian (a heresy), "holding many and awful errors."
- Formosus, 891 AD, was guilty of perjury.
- Stephen VII 896 AD, entered like a thief and died by the rope.
- John XII, 956 AD, tried and found guilty of blasphemy, perjury, sacrilege, adultery, incest, and murder,

- Benedict IX, 1053 AD, a boy-pope, created at the age of ten or twelve years, spent his days in debauchery, rapine, and murder.
- Boniface VIII, 1294 AD, denied the Trinity, the Incarnation, and the immortality of the soul.
- John XXIII, deposed by the Council of Constance, was a rank infidel and was convicted of crimes in which the indictment "contained all mortal sins, and infinity of abominations." Prior to his stint as Pope, he had been a Neopolitan pirate with his two brothers. (Elaboration below.)
- Alexander VI, 1492 AD, prepared poison for others and drank it by mistake.

The above are quoted from *Handbook on Popery, A History of the Council of Trent*, pp. 71-72, J. D. Cramp, Houlston & Company, London, 1851

Here are some elaborations and examples from another source:

Popess Joan, 855 AD: Asserted to be a myth by some, still others with as good or better reputation maintain that this lady was Popess, "la Papessa." Among the advocates for it being the truth, are Petrarch, in his *Lives of the Pope* (Petrarch was a Roman Catholic and friend of a Pope); and John Charles Gerson, (Chancellor of the University of Paris in the fifteenth century, and titled "most Christian Doctor" by the Roman Catholic Church).

As to Formosus, he was excommunicated for murder, but elected Pope in 891 AD. He died five years later. His replacement, Boniface VI, reigned for only 15 days and was replaced by Stephen VII. Stephen exhumed the rotting body of Formosas, dressed him in Papal vestments, sat him in a chair and tried him for his crimes. At the end of this trial, the "holy" vestments were removed, and three of his fingers cut off and his body was cast into the Tiber River. Stephen was taken captive by the opposition party, thrown into the dungeon and strangled.

John XXIII above was known as Cardinal Balthassar Cosa prior to becoming pope. He became the self-appointed Pope through threat of physical force. Dressed as a corsair (pirate) and in possession of the meeting place, he proclaimed himself Pope. At this point he murdered many that might have been a threat to him. Murder was not a stranger to this brigand. In his early days he joined a band of pirates and became their leader in committing terrible atrocities. He was a man "destitute of faith, shame, and remorse."

Taken from *Is the Roman Church 'Holy,'* by H.A. Henderson, published by Charles Thynne, London, 1914. (A more detailed listing of the fruit of the Popes is in the appendix at the end of this book.)

If there was an apostolic succession, and if that succession was to create the Roman Catholic Church, God would only have godly men become leaders. Consider Hophni and Phinehas, the sons of Eli the Priest in Israel.

> Now the sons of Eli were base men; they knew not Jehovah. And the custom of the priests with the people was, that, when any man offered sacrifice, the priest's servant came, while the flesh was boiling, with a flesh-hook of three teeth in his hand; and he struck it into the pan, or kettle, or caldron, or pot; all that the flesh-hook brought up the priest took therewith. So they did in Shiloh unto all the Israelites that came thither. Yea, before they burnt the fat, the priest's servant came, and said to the man that sacrificed, "Give flesh to roast for the priest; for he will not have boiled flesh of thee, but raw." And if the man said unto him, "They will surely burn the fat first, and then take as much as thy soul desireth;" then he would say, "Nay, but thou shalt give it me now: and if not, I will take it by force." And the sin of the young men was very great before Jehovah; for the men despised the offering of Jehovah (1 Samuel 2:12-17 ASV).
>
> Now Eli was very old; and he heard all that his sons did unto all Israel, and how that they lay with the women that did service at the door of the tent of meeting. And he said unto them, "Why do ye such things? for I hear of your evil dealings from all this people. Nay, my sons; for it is no good report that I hear: ye make Jehovah's people to transgress. If one man sin against another, God shall judge him; but if a man sin against Jehovah, who shall entreat for him?" Notwithstanding, they hearkened not unto the voice of their father, because Jehovah was minded to slay them (1 Samuel 2:22-25 ASV).
>
> And there came a man of God unto Eli, and said unto him, "Thus saith Jehovah, 'Did I reveal myself unto the house of thy father, when they were in Egypt *in bondage* to Pharaoh's house? and did I choose him out of all the tribes of Israel to be my priest, to go up unto mine altar, to burn incense, to wear an ephod before me? and did I give unto the house of thy father all the offerings of the children of Israel made by fire? Wherefore kick ye at my sacrifice and at mine offering, which I have commanded in my habitation, and honorest thy sons above me, to make yourselves fat with the chiefest of all the offerings of Israel my people?' Therefore Jehovah, the God of Israel, saith, 'I said indeed that thy house, and the house of thy father, should walk before me for ever:' but now Jehovah saith, 'Be it far from me; for them that honor me I will honor, and they that despise me shall be lightly esteemed. Behold, the days come, that I will cut off thine arm, and the arm of thy father's house, that there shall not be an old man in thy house'" (1 Samuel 2:27-31 ASV).

As you see, the sins of Eli's sons were great. Further, Eli sinned in that he would not discipline them, but let them do as they wanted. The sons were eventually killed, and the house of Eli died out.

The Word of God says that God will not be lightly regarded. We saw this with Adam's sin. If the Roman Church was intended to be the Church of the Living God through apostolic succession, the Popes previously cited would not have existed. These are but a sampling of popes with disgusting and criminal behavior down through the two thousand years since Christ walked the path between Galilee and Jerusalem.

Escape From Paganism

The Sacraments

As a Roman Catholic these are things that you must believe about the sacraments in general:

- All were instituted by Jesus Christ.
- There are seven sacraments: baptism, confirmation, the eucharist, penance, extreme unction, order, and matrimony.
- These are sacraments of the New Law and differ from the sacraments of the Old Law.
- No sacrament is of greater value than any of the others.
- These sacraments are necessary to salvation; you cannot be saved without them.
- The sacraments are not limited to nourishing faith alone.
- The sacraments both contain and convey God's grace, and New Law grace.
- The right to preach and teach the Word of God is restricted.
- One must do what the Roman Church intends when administering the sacraments.

As stated above, you must believe all of the above about the sacraments, generally, or you are anathema. What does "anathema" mean? It means that you are accursed, or damned.

Here is a surprise quiz for you. It is an easy, one question quiz. What is it that got Adam in trouble, and thereby all of us? The answer is that Adam did not believe what God said, and rebelled against Him.

There is another aspect to this problem. It is the aspect of adding to God's Word. This is attributing something to God, as having said or done something that He did not say or do. Here are a couple of verses that relate to this.

> You shall not add unto the word which I command you, neither shall ye diminish from it, that ye may keep the commandments of Jehovah your God which I command you (Deuteronomy 4:2 ASV).
>
> I testify unto every man that heareth the words of the prophecy of this book, if any man shall add unto them, God shall add unto him the plagues which are written in this book: and if any man shall take away from the words of the book of this prophecy, God shall take away his part from the tree of life, and out of the holy city, which are written in this book (Revelations 22:18-19 ASV).

You can search your Bible; you will not find the word, or the concept of sacrament in the Bible. This is something that has been added by false teachers to the Word of God. It is the clay telling the Potter what is right. Sacramentarianism is rebellion against the living God, just as much as was Adam's unbelief!

The Bible is complete. It is all that God has determined to reveal to us for these days. If you add something to God's revelation, you will suffer eternal destruction. That is what it means to have your part in the Tree of Life revoked.

Here is a quote from the *International Standard Bible Encyclopedia*. It is available at:
http://www.bible-history.com/isbe/S/SACRAMENTS.

> The word "sacrament" comes from the Latin sacramentum, which in the classical period of the language was used in two chief senses: (1) as a legal term to denote the sum of money deposited by two parties to a suit which was forfeited by the loser and appropriated to sacred uses; (2) as a military term to designate the oath of obedience taken by newly enlisted soldiers. Whether referring to an oath of obedience or to something set apart for a sacred purpose, it is evident that sacramentum would readily lend itself to describe such ordinances as Baptism and the Lord's Supper. In the Greek New Testament, however, there is no word, nor even any general idea corresponding to "sacrament," nor does the earliest history of Christianity afford any trace of the application of the term to certain rites of the church. Pliny (circa 112 AD) describes the Christians of Bithynia as "binding themselves by a sacramentum to commit no kind of crime" (Epistles x.97), but scholars are now pretty generally agreed that Pliny here uses the word in its old Roman sense of an oath or solemn obligation, so that its occurrence in this passage is nothing more than an interesting coincidence.

Well into the second century after Christ, the concept of sacraments for church ritual is unknown. It was not until the end of the second century and the beginning of the third that the concept of sacraments is first seen. Tertullian mentions the term in connection with baptism and the eucharist.

The term "sacrament" was used in the early Latin Bible to translate the Greek word "musterion," or mystery. The Latin Bible preceeded, and was the basis of the Vulgate. Neither Bibles were an accurate translation from either the Hebrew Old Testament or the Greek New Testament. The cites for this claim (where the term "mystery" is translated "sacrament") are Ephesians 5:32, which refers to Christ and the Church; First Timothy 3:16, a reference to Christ; Revelations 1:20, which is a reference to the seven churches to which the first part of the Book of Revelations is addressed. Here is Ephesians 5:32 from the *Latin Vulgate:*

sacramentum hoc magnum est ego autem dico in
Christo et in ecclesia.

The word "sacramentum" is the word mystery and it refers to Christ and the "ecclesia" or church. Nothing, absolutely nothing, in the Bible, let alone the citations above, refers to the seven sacraments imposed by the Roman Church.

Finally Revelation 17:7 refers to what many people, including me, think refers to the Roman Church and the resuscitated Roman Empire in the final days of the period called the Tribulation. This will be just before the return of Christ as King to begin His millennial reign upon the earth. Christ reveals this to John as a "mystery," not as a sacrament.

Those who translated these references into Latin chose a word that was not even close to the meaning of the word "mystery." The term "mystery" does not refer to a pledge. The Latin term "sacrament" does refer to a pledge. Why did they do this? The evidence that they could translate indicates their "mistake" was intentional. It would seem they had a non-biblical agenda.

The concept of sacrament has nothing to do with the teachings of true Christianity. It has to do with the adulteration of Christianity. The sacraments were put in place to help assimilate

Christianity with the mystery religions of the then Greek/Roman world.

The Latin meaning of "sacrament" was redefined by the time Augustine wrote in the fourth century. He defined the term as meaning "a visible form of invisible grace." This same explanation was adopted by the Council of Trent, who added: "and became its channel." The "channel" of grace, that is.

St. Hugo, writing in the twelfth century, enumerated 30 sacraments recognized by the Roman Church. The Council of Trent backed this off to seven. Is there not some confusion here about the infallibility of the Roman Church?

> God is not a man, that he should lie, Neither the son of man, that he should repent: Hath he said, and will he not do it? Or hath he spoken, and will he not make it good? (Numbers 23:19 ASV).

> For I am God, and there is none else; I am God, and there is none like me; declaring the end from the beginning, and from ancient times things that are not yet done; saying, My counsel shall stand, and I will do all my pleasure (Isaiah 46:10 ASV).

> The grass withereth, the flower fadeth; but the word of our God shall stand forever (Isaiah 40:8 ASV).

God is infallible. If the sacraments were really from Him, He would not have had thirty sacraments one day and seven the next. They are not from God and those that established them, support them, teach them, and practice them, are of the first Adam. If you are one of the above, please examine your relationship with God today, while there is still time!

What about the issue of a sacrament being the channel of grace? Does grace require an act or ritual for its conveyance?

What Is Grace?

What is Grace?

Grace is: God's Riches at Christ's Expense (G.R.A.C.E.). Grace is the action of a superior to an inferior who has no real claim for gracious treatment. In fact, the inferior deserves the opposite.

The recipient of grace receives the riches of God because he or she believes that Christ's death was for his/her sin. They have believed that Christ died for them so that they could be forgiven their sin.

Grace is not a force. Grace is a decision. Grace does not require a conveyance; grace is a decision to allow, or permit. Grace is the decision upon God's part to allow unmerited favor to those who believe.

God determines grace upon all those who believe in His Son as their Savior and Lord (alone), thereby allowing them new and eternal life. Christ's death and resurrection purchased it for them. God, in determining grace for them forgets their sin. Eternal means forever, with no vacant spots, or interruptions!

Other gifts are determined upon the believer for service to Christ's body, the Church. It is true that these gifts are called (charismata), a word derived from the term grace. These are gifts bestowed upon the believer by the Holy Spirit to the believer's heart. These are not conveyed by ritual. For example:

> Now concerning spiritual gifts, brethren, I would not have you ignorant. Ye know that when ye were Gentiles ye were led away unto those dumb idols, howsoever ye might led. Wherefore I make known unto you, that no man speaking in the Spirit of God saith, "Jesus is anathema;" and no man can say, "Jesus is Lord," but in the Holy Spirit. Now there are diversities of gifts, but the same Spirit. And there are diversities of ministrations, and the same Lord. And there are diversities of workings, but the same God, who worketh all things in all. But to each one is given the manifestation of the Spirit to profit withal (1 Corinthians 12:1-7 ASV).

We see here that the "channel" for the conveyance of the gifts is God the Holy Spirit. God does not require special rituals, such as baptism, the eucharist/mass, or others to channel His grace to us. Nor has He determined to do so. The Roman Church asserts this, but asserts it falsely. There is nothing in the Bible that supports this claim.

Certainly, Canon One of the section on Sacraments in the *Roman Catholic Catechism* is false, and a known lie when it was established. It states that:

> **Canon 1.** If anyone saith that the sacraments of the New Law were not all instituted by Jesus Christ our Lord ... let him be anathema (*Dogmatic Canons and Decrees,* Devin-Adair Company, 1912 and Page 54, *Canons & Decrees of the Council of Trent,* Rev. J. Waterworth, Page 89).

Jesus Christ did not institute these sacraments. They were not even talked about until about 200 years after His death and resurrection. Since anathema means damned, does not the Roman Catholic catechism thereby damn Christ? Is not the clay sitting in judgment of the Potter? They refer to "anyone;" surely Christ is an "anyone?"

As we saw in the passage from 1 Corinthians, no one can call Jesus accursed by the Holy Spirit. Since Jesus Christ, Himself, did not institute the sacraments, He certainly would not believe that He did. Therefore, according to Canon 1, Romans label Him as anathema, which means accursed or damned. We will see that is the case with the other sacraments also. They actually damn God. They do not damn Him by the Holy Spirit, but by that fiendish creature, Satan.

To be in compliance with canon one on the sacraments, one must practice and believe in the New Law and the Mosaic Law. Those who do not, are damned, accursed, anathema.

New Law

There is a wonderful resource on the internet at www.archive.org. Among its assets is a library of e-books that relate to theological and historical issues. These are all old books that have been scanned and made available. Many of them are excellent resources written by first-class scholars. There is a wealth of information there with viewpoints from all angles. I recommend that you pay this site a visit.

Two of the hundreds of books I downloaded are Roman Catholic catechisms generated by the Roman Church. They are out of print, so if you wish to verify the truth of what I write here, visit the site.

The books are *Dogmatic Canons and Decrees* published by Devin-Adair Company in New York (1912), and *The Canons and Decrees of the Sacred and Oecumenical Council of Trent* by Rev. J. Waterworth (which also contains a history of the Council). This book was published by the Catholic Publication Society Company in New York in 1848.

"Old books" we might be inclined to say. "Things have maybe changed."

I think not. The Canons of the Council of Trent were reaffirmed by Vatican II. The Church claims to be infallible, does it not? We have seen that it is not infallible, haven't we? Yet it sticks to its guns in claiming infallibility. So, how could it change? If it made no mistakes, nothing needs changing; "if it ain't broke, don't fix it." If you are infallible you cannot need repair.

What have these to do with "New Law?" Just this, if you download a copy of either book or count the number of Canons (laws) attached to the sacraments, the total is 150. The "New Law" is to be followed in addition to the Mosaic Law and in violation of God's Word. God, in His Word, says that the

Mosaic Law is done away with. The **New Covenant** has replaced it. As to this New Law, no comment is made in the Bible, as it is not of God.

We need to look at what God has said about the Mosaic Law. The points made concerning it also apply to any other legalistic imposition made on the members of His Son's Body, the Church.

> Yet knowing that a man is not justified by the works of the law but through faith in Jesus Christ, even we believed on Christ Jesus, that we might be justified by faith in Christ, and not by the works of the law: because by the works of the law shall no flesh be justified (Galatians 2:16 ASV).

> For as many as are of the works of the law are under a curse: for it is written, "Cursed is every one who continueth not in all things that are written in the book of the law, to do them." Now that no man is justified by the law before God, is evident: for, The righteous shall live by faith (Galatians 3:10-11 ASV).

Look at these verses well. Pick up that Bible laying there and read the Book of Galatians three or four times. Ask God to make you understand what it is saying. It is very important.

In the Roman Catholic catechism, members are told they are under the Mosaic Law. Further, on the pain of being damned (anathematized), they must believe in, and practice, the New Law. Yet, if you will closely read the passage from Galatians 3:10-11, God says that if you are under the law (Mosaic Law as in the Ten Commandments fame) you are cursed, which means anathematized or damned. Are you obedient to Roman Catholic teachings? If so, it says here you are damned! Not a comforting thought, is it?

Remember, salvation is by faith in Christ, not the performance of magical or legalistic rituals.

Sacrament of Baptism

T**he Greek word *baptisma*** (our word baptism) means to dip into or immerse.

Let's start with the standard for defining such things, the Bible. It is God's Owner's Manual, and the most important Book in creation. It is truth from God, who is truth. It is truth that is far above nature and is revealed by God. It is God's instructions, which man could never reason out because they are above man's physical or natural ability to investigate. The Bible is of God.

Baptism shows up first in Scripture as an activity being practiced by John the Baptist. What was the purpose of John's baptizing?

> John answered them, saying, "I baptize in water: in the midst of you standeth one whom ye know not, even he that cometh after me, the latchet of whose shoe I am not worthy to unloose." These things were done in Bethany beyond the Jordan, where John was baptizing. On the morrow he seeth Jesus coming unto him, and saith, "Behold, the Lamb of God, that taketh away the sin of the world! This is he of whom I said, 'After me cometh a man who is become before me: for he was before me. And I knew him not; but that he should be made manifest to Israel, for this cause came I baptizing in water.'" And John bare witness, saying, "I have beheld the Spirit descending as a dove out of heaven; and it abode upon him. And I knew him not: but he that sent me to baptize in water, he said unto me, 'Upon whomsoever thou shalt see the Spirit descending, and abiding upon him, the same is he that baptizeth in the Holy Spirit.' And I have seen, and have borne witness that this is the Son of God" (John 1:26-34 ASV).

John the Baptist made two points relevant to our discussion:

1. His purpose for baptizing was to manifest, reveal, or show, to Israel, their Messiah, Jesus Christ.

2. That Christ would baptize in the Holy Spirit. John 4:2 states that Jesus was **not** baptizing (in water); only His disciples.

> And in those days cometh John the Baptist, preaching in the wilderness of Judaea, saying, "Repent ye; for the kingdom of heaven is at hand. For this is he that was spoken of through Isaiah the prophet, saying, 'The voice of one crying in the wilderness, Make ye ready the way

of the Lord, Make his paths straight.'" Now John himself had his raiment of camel's hair, and a leathern girdle about his loins; and his food was locusts and wild honey. Then went out unto him Jerusalem, and all Judaea, and the entire region round about the Jordan; and they were baptized of him in the river Jordan, confessing their sins. But when he saw many of the Pharisees and Sadducees coming to his baptism, he said unto them, "Ye offspring of vipers, who warned you to flee from the wrath to come? Bring forth therefore fruit worthy of repentance: and think not to say within yourselves, 'We have Abraham to our father:' for I say unto you, that God is able of these stones to raise up children unto Abraham. And even now the axe lieth at the root of the trees: every tree therefore that bringeth not forth good fruit is hewn down, and cast into the fire. I indeed baptize you in water unto repentance: but he that cometh after me is mightier than I, whose shoes I am not worthy to bear: he shall baptize you in the Holy Spirit and in fire: whose fan is in his hand, and he will thoroughly cleanse his threshing-floor; and he will gather his wheat into the garner, but the chaff he will burn up with unquenchable fire" (Matthew 3:1-12 ASV).

Here we see John affirming that He baptizes to reveal the Lord by reciting a prophesy written 700 years earlier: "Make ready the way of the Lord, Make His paths straight." John goes on to say that the Lord will baptize with the **Holy Spirit and Fire.** John's baptism was not to salvation. It was a preachment to call out that those being baptized needed to repent. How do we know this? John points out that Christ will baptize either with the Holy Spirit or Fire. Those baptized by the Spirit will be saved; those baptized with Fire are the damned.

Baptism of the Holy Spirit refers to unification with Christ by being baptized into the Spirit, or placed into Christ's body, the Church. The baptism of fire refers to the eternal judgment all unbelievers will receive at the great White Throne when they suffer the second death and are sentenced to eternity in the Lake of Fire, where there will be constant weeping and gnashing of teeth.

From this introduction let's advance to what the Roman Catholic Church says about it. There are 14 Canons or items of the New Law associated with this sacrament. We will not cover them all, only the ones relevant to the discussion in this book. (Keep in mind that the word anathema means to be accursed or damned.)

> **Canon II:** If anyone saith that true and natural water is not of necessity for baptism, and, on that account, wrest, to some sort of metaphor, those words of our lord Jesus Christ: Unless a man be born again of water and the Holy Ghost: let him be anathema.

John the Baptist stated that Christ would baptize with the Spirit and Fire. It would appear that the Roman Catholic Church has damned John the Baptist. Am I confused? Have they not made him a Saint?

> **Canon III:** If anyone saith that the Roman Church, which is the mother and mistress of all churches, there is not the true doctrine concerning the sacrament of baptism; let him be anathema.
>
> **Canon V:** If anyone saith that baptism is optional, that is, not necessary unto salvation; let him be anathema.
>
> **Canon VII:** If anyone saith that the baptized are, by baptism itself, made debtors but to faith alone, and not to the observance of the whole law of Christ, let him be anathema.
>
> **Canon VIII:** If anyone saith that the baptized are freed from all the precepts, whether written or transmitted of the Holy Church, in such wise that they are not bound to observe them, unless they have chosen of their own accord to submit themselves thereunto, let him be anathema.

Starting with Canon II, the Roman Church teaches that John 3:5 teaches that baptism must be with water. What I understand to be the biblical position is that born of water refers to natural birth. This position is stated in context. Here is the entire passage:

> Jesus answered, "Verily, verily, I say unto thee, Except one be born of water and the Spirit, he cannot enter into the kingdom of God! That which is born of the flesh is flesh; and that which is born of the Spirit is spirit. Marvel not that I said unto thee, Ye must be born anew. The wind bloweth where it will, and thou hearest the voice thereof, but knowest not whence it cometh, and whither it goeth: so is every one that is born of the Spirit" (John 3:5-8 ASV).

As you see, 3:5 talks about being born of water, not baptized in water, born of the water and of the Spirit. The first is natural birth, and the second is of the Spirit sent by Christ to make you into a new creation.

This passage clearly states that to be admitted in to the Kingdom of God, first one must be born naturally (of water=the water bag), just like we were all born. Here is something obvious to consider, if one is not born, one does not exist. Seems elementary, doesn't it?

It goes on to say that one must be regenerated by the Spirit of God, born again of the Spirit. So, first, we are of the earth, earthy, a descendant of the first Adam. Then we are of the Spirit, a descendant of the second Adam, Jesus Christ, and united to Him. When regenerated by the Spirit, we become a spiritual person, still dragging around this body of flesh, but soon to be rid of it.

The issue of the "natural" verses the "spiritual" is reiterated by the Apostle Paul in 1 Corinthians 15:44-49 (ASV):

> it is sown a natural body; it is raised a spiritual body. If there is a natural body, there is also a spiritual body. So also it is written, The first man Adam became a living soul. The last Adam became a life-giving spirit. Howbeit that is not first which is spiritual, but that which is natural; then that which is spiritual. The first man is of the earth, earthy: the second man is of heaven. As is the earthy, such are they also that are earthy: and as is the heavenly, such are they also that are heavenly. And as we have borne the image of the earthy, we shall also bear the image of the heavenly.

A sensible rule about reading is that we should always take a word to mean what it is normally intended to mean. Do not be like Humpty Dumpty, and make words mean whatever you want them to mean. God, who has wisdom, knowledge, and intelligence far above ours, has chosen to communicate to lowly man. He has done it with words that dumb man can understand. God intends to communicate His instructions to us and intends for us to understand. So we must take Him at His Word, that is, what He intends and He will bring us to understand if we do not twist His Word into something unintended.

False theologians have twisted the word "born" to mean "baptism." They are guilty of unbelief just as was the first Adam, when he sinned the very first time. Canon II used the phrase "born again of water and the Holy Spirit." In Canon II they have deliberately changed God's Word as John 3:5 does not say this. It is that passage they seem to be quoting. Using the **Catholic Study Bible** that verse says: "I say unto you, no one can enter the kingdom of God without being born of water and Spirit" (John 3:5). Note that "born again" is not part of verse 5. The Roman Church has committed a deliberate and obvious falsehood here, as nowhere else in the Bible is such a statement or inference made!

Notice in Canon II, like the other canons, if **anyone** does not believe that Jesus required baptism in the John 3:5 passage, and if anyone does not believe that natural water is required, that person is "anathema" or damned. Is not the man, Christ Jesus, an **anyone**? Is not the **God/Man**, Christ Jesus an **anyone**? Clearly the Roman Catholic Church has **damned** Christ as nowhere in the Bible is it taught that one is saved by the act of baptism.

This is rather shocking, but true. Many of the Canons of the Catholic Catechism damn God!

Since Canon II is false, so are the others that relate to this "sacrament." Canon III is obviously false since Canon II is false.

Consider Canon VIII.

> **Canon VIII:** If anyone saith that the baptized are freed from all the precepts, whether written or transmitted of the Holy Church, in such wise that they are not bound to observe them, unless they have chosen of their own accord to submit themselves thereunto, let him be anathema.

The concept of precepts refers to law. The laws referred to are both the Mosaic Law (Ten Commandments, etc.) and the New Law established by Rome. They really miss the issue here and reject Scripture.

The New Man, the second Adam, is under the **New Covenant** and **not** under the Law of Moses or the canon law of Rome, titled the New Law.

> Behold, the days come, saith Jehovah, that I will make a new covenant with the house of Israel, and with the house of Judah: not according to the covenant that I made with their fathers in the day that I took them by the hand to bring them out of the land of Egypt; which my covenant they brake, although I was a husband unto them, saith Jehovah. But this is the covenant that I will make with the house of Israel after those days, saith Jehovah: I will put my law in their inward parts, and in their heart will I write it; and I will be their God, and they shall be my people: and they shall teach no more every man his neigh-

> bor, and every man his brother, saying, Know Jehovah; for they shall all know me, from the least of them unto the greatest of them, saith Jehovah: for I will forgive their iniquity, and their sin will I remember no more (Jeremiah 31:31-34 ASV).

> So then, my beloved, even as ye have always obeyed, not as in my presence only, but now much more in my absence, work out your own salvation with fear and trembling; for it is God who worketh in you both to will and to work, for his good pleasure (Philippians 2:12-13 ASV).

Under the **New Covenant**, it is the Holy Spirit within the believer that changes the believer's "wanter" from evil to good. It is God changing the believer into an obedient servant. This process is called sanctification. Man by this returns to using the image of God for God.

A covenant is a contract or promise. It is either bilateral (requires performance by two or more parties) or unilateral, requiring performance by only one party. The New Covenant is a contract by God with man and it requires performance by God alone. Man is passive as regards to this covenant. The performance is of God and upon those to whom He wills, those who have placed their faith in Christ Jesus as Savior and Lord. Let it be said, **in Christ alone!**

Understand that we are saved only by faith. Jesus says this specifically in John 3:16-17 (ASV): "For God so loved the world, that he gave his only begotten Son, that whosoever believeth on him should not perish, but have eternal life. For God sent not the Son into the world to judge the world; but that the world should be saved through him."

In the Gospel of John, alone, there are at least fifteen passages that attribute eternal life to belief in Jesus Christ. There is not even one that attributes eternal life to the sacrament of baptism.

Close your eyes for a moment and imagine you are outside the Temple in Jerusalem some 2,000 years ago. Thousands of people are milling around, when suddenly these strange men get up and start speaking, each in a different language. You came here to celebrate the Jewish day of Pentecost. What is happening?

You can read about this event in Acts 2:37-41 (ASV):

ESCAPE FROM PAGANISM

> Now when they heard this, they were pricked in their heart, and said unto Peter and the rest of the apostles, Brethren, what shall we do? And Peter said unto them, Repent ye, and be baptized every one of you in the name of Jesus Christ unto the remission of your sins; and ye shall receive the gift of the Holy Spirit. For to you is the promise, and to your children, and to all that are afar off, even as many as the Lord our God shall call unto him. And with many other words he testified, and exhorted them, saying, Save yourselves from this crooked generation. They then that received his word were baptized: and there were added unto them in that day about three thousand souls.

If you quickly read the above you **might** say that the principle steps here to salvation are:

Repent, and

Be Baptized

For the forgiveness of your sins.

If you do, then you are missing the most important part and that is the part about the three thousand believing.

In the first place, consider the word "repent." It means to turn from. In context it means to turn from sin to Christ. This involves belief. You will not turn if you do not believe you need to. So here is evidence of "belief."

The primary evidence of belief, though, is the first verse where the three thousand believed (cut to the heart) that they had crucified their Lord and Christ (Messiah). They had just experienced the convicting work of the Spirit (see John 16:5). The Holy Spirit had just enlightened them as to the truth of their sinfulness and need for the Savior. They had just been regenerated and now would repent. Think of it, regenerated, they had a new heart. By the work of the Holy Spirit, truth had been shed in their hearts and they now saw truth. What else could they do but repent? With this vision and the wonderful news of gaining life eternal, they were baptized to identify with Jesus Christ, of whose body (the church) they were now part of.

Here is the path of salvation that is explained in the Pentecost passage:

Conviction by the Holy Spirit,

Belief in the Truth, that Christ died for their sin,

Repentance of their sin,

Baptized to identify with the death and resurrection of our Lord Jesus Christ.

This was the formula then and now. It hasn't changed.

Belief, not baptism, brings salvation. The very idea of baptismal regeneration did not begin until about 100 years after the crucifixion of our Lord. It was a perversion in practice brought on by fear. Fear that infants, the sick and dying might not go to heaven unless something was done to convert them. It was a sinful fear of God, that He would not do the right thing as regards these infants. So with the belief that some mechanical, magical, ritual might work, baptism was settled on. It is a perversion of the Word of God. I keep harping on this, but remember the trouble the first Adam got us into when he perverted the Word of God?

> Seven effects of baptism are enumerated by the compilers of the "Catechism." It is said to "remit original sin and actual guilt, however enormous;" to remit all the punishment due to sin; to bestow invaluable privileges, such as justification and adoption; to produce abundance of virtues; to unite the soul to Christ; to seal it with an ineffaceable character; and to open the portals of heaven (*Catechism Council of Trent* pp.127-132 (Donlevy) by JD Cramp in *Handbook on Popery* p. 164).

The remission of sin, though, is only for sins already committed. Any sin committed subsequent to baptism needs to be expiated by penance. When we get to the section on penance, we will see that the Priest replaces God. We have already seen how Catholic sacraments damn Christ and God.

This is ludicrous! The "seven effects of Baptism" are lies. We will not find them in God's Word. These "effects" do not exist in reality anymore than the subject matter recorded in the *Fairy Tales of the Mother Goose Rhymes.*

> For God so loved the world, that he gave his only begotten Son, that whosoever believeth on him should not perish, but have eternal life. For God sent not the Son into the world to judge the world; but that

the world should be saved through him. He that believeth on him is not judged: he that believeth not hath been judged already, because he hath not believed on the name of the only begotten Son of God (John 3:16-18 ASV).

Salvation is by faith and faith alone, in Christ alone, through God's grace alone, as revealed in Scripture alone–not through baptism.

> For by grace have ye been saved through faith; and that not of yourselves, it is the gift of God; not of works, that no man should glory (Ephesians 2:8-9 ASV).

Sacrament of Penance

Penance is a ritual designed for sinners to regain the salvation imparted to them by baptism, which was lost with sin. It is a depiction of the Jack and Jill rhyme expressed earlier. Man sins constantly. In 1 John 1:8, John wrote: "If we say we have no sin the truth is not in us." For myself, I will say that I would probably have to devote my life, 24 hours per day, and seven days per week, to doing penance, because before I was through with one penance I would have several more to do as I would have sinned again while doing the one. In fact, I might get dizzy trying to get out of the church having to turn around and around and around, before reaching the door, repeatedly going back to the confessional booth and getting a new penance. Whew!

Remember, sin can be committed in our thoughts, words, or deeds. Read the second chapter of 2 Peter for examples.

Here is what the Roman Church says about penance.

> If such, in all the regenerate, were their gratitude towards God as that they constantly preserved the justice received in Baptism by His bounty and grace, there would not have been need for another sacrament besides that of Baptism itself to be instituted for the remission of sins (canon II). But because God, rich in mercy, knows our frame, He has bestowed a remedy of life even on those who may, after Baptism, have delivered themselves up to the servitude of sin and the power of the devil, –The Sacrament, to wit, of Penance, by which the benefit of the death of Christ is applied to those who have fallen after Baptism. Penitence was indeed at all times necessary, in order to attain to grace and justice for all men who had defiled themselves of any mortal sin, even for those who begged to be washed by the Sacrament of Baptism; that so, their perverseness renounced and amended, they might, with a hatred of sin and a godly sorrow of mind, detest so great an offense of God (*Dogmatic Canons and Decrees of The Council Trent;* Devon-Adair Co., Pages 86-87).

This sacrament is an outright lie! Well, so are the others, so what is new? In establishing this sacrament, the Roman Church has clearly stated yes to the question: Est Homo Deus? Is man God? Let's look at the assertions this one makes and measure it against what God says in the Bible. This strikes at the heart of what it means to be a Christian. Here are the three main points raised above.

Man does not preserve the justice received in baptism.

- Penitence has always been necessary to attain grace and justice for all who had defiled themselves of any mortal sin.
- Since this is so, some additional means was needed for the remission of sins committed after baptism,
- Men, after salvific baptism, deliver themselves back into the servitude and power of the Devil

PRESERVING JUSTICE RECEIVED IN BAPTISM:

It is alleged by the Roman Church that you can be saved by baptism. You see that they teach that justice is received in baptism. Justice! Understand what justice is. The Roman Church is confounding it with salvation and grace as we see in the following. Let's consider the two main terms used, justice and grace, plus the one inferred salvation.

Grace

> Now to him that worketh, the reward is not reckoned as of grace, but as of debt. But to him that worketh not, but believeth on him that justifieth the ungodly, his faith is reckoned for righteousness. Even as David also pronounceth blessing upon the man, unto whom God reckoneth righteousness apart from works (Romans 4:4-6 ASV).

> Even so then at this present time also there is a remnant according to the election of grace. But if it is by grace, it is no more of works: otherwise grace is no more grace (Romans 11:5-6 ASV).

Here we see that works are the opposite of grace. The very nature of penance is works. Penance is opposed to grace. The sacrament destroys God's grace. Penance is a ritual that is anti-Christ. One of the best ways to understand grace is an acronym: G.R.A.C.E., which stands for "God's riches at Christ's expense." Because of the life, death, and resurrection of Jesus Christ, God can exercise or bestow, justly, His mercy and grace upon whom He chooses.

Justice

Justice is a legal concept or term. To be "just" one must be right, or righteous. If he/she is not, then that person is not just. That person may receive justice, and that justice would be a penalty. All mankind is guilty of sin, corporately and individually. Man is guilty before God of trying to replace the Triune God of Heaven, with the triune god of earth: "Me, Myself, and I." Is man God? The justice for this is the penalty of death, not salvation.

No mechanical, or "magical" ritual such as penance can overcome this penalty

- The act of forgiving crime cannot be the application of justice. The act has to be one of mercy and grace.

- God, through His mercy and grace does **justify** those who have believed in Christ. This justification is because of the works of Christ and through the regeneration of the sinner. The sinner is made a "new creation." He/she is no longer the man of flesh, but a new spiritual person. The Spirit of God now indwells the "new creation" molding and changing him/her into a godly character.

> Wherefore we henceforth know no man after the flesh: even though we have known Christ after the flesh, yet now we know him so no more. Wherefore if any man is in Christ, he is a new creature: the old things are passed away; behold, they are become new. But all things are of God, who reconciled us to himself through Christ, and gave unto us the ministry of reconciliation; to wit, that God was in Christ reconciling the world unto himself, not reckoning unto them their trespasses, and having committed unto us the word of reconciliation. We are ambassadors therefore on behalf of Christ, as though God were entreating by us: we beseech you on behalf of Christ, be ye reconciled to God. Him who knew no sin he made to be sin on our behalf; that we might become the righteousness of God in him (2 Corinthians 5:16-21 ASV).

Notice that the righteousness (justice) referred to above relates to God, not man.

SALVATION:

Salvation is permanent. It consists of at least these things:

- Spiritual conviction or enlightenment: the Holy Spirit makes you see that you are a sinner in need of Christ (see John 16:8-9).
- Faith that God gives through His grace, "For by grace you have been saved through faith and that not of yourself, it is a gift of God, not of works, that no man should glory" (Ephesians 2:8-9).
- Born of the Spirit (see John 3:5-6).
- Justified by God because of the finished work of Christ on our behalf.
- Being sanctified (see Philippians 1:6 & 2:12-13, Romans 8).
- Glorified: "When we see Him we will be like Him" (1 John 3:2).

If we are truly a child of God, we are a member of a new race of man. It is the race of the second Adam. We are a new creation. We are not un-recreated each time we sin and then have to run back to the old "re-creation mixer" at the church to get whipped back into shape. God will discipline us and work on us from within. We will be changed. Our "wanter" will be conformed to God's wants and not ours. God is at work, not us. It cannot be us because we are a part of that group defined in Romans 3:23: "there is none righteous, no not one; all fall short of the glory of God."

> Now we know that what things soever the law saith, it speaketh to them that are under the law; that every mouth may be stopped, and all the world may be brought under the judgment of God: because by the works of the law shall no flesh be justified in his sight; for through the law cometh the knowledge of sin. But now apart from the law a righteousness of God hath been manifested, being witnessed by the law and the prophets, being witnessed by the law and the prophets; even the righteousness of God through faith in Jesus Christ unto all them that believe; for there is no distinction; for all have sinned, and fall short of the glory of God; being justified freely by his grace through

the redemption that is in Christ Jesus: whom God set forth to be a propitiation, through faith, in his blood, to show his righteousness because of the passing over of the sins done aforetime, in the forbearance of God; for the showing, I say, of his righteousness at this present season: that he might himself be just, and the justifier of him that hath faith in Jesus (Romans 3:19-26 ASV).

Here are some of the Canons established at Trent relating to Penance:

Canon 1: If anyone says that in the Catholic Church Penance is not truly and properly a sacrament, instituted by Christ the Lord for reconciling the faithful unto God, as often as the fall into sin after baptism; let him be anathema [accursed, damned]

Canon III: If anyone says that those words of the Lord the Saviour: "Receive ye the Holy Ghost, whose sins you shall forgive, they are forgiven them, and whose sins you shall retain, they are retained," are not to be understood of the power of forgiving and of retaining in the sacrament of Penance, as the Catholic Church has always from the beginning understood them; but wrests them, contrary to the institution of this sacrament, to the power of preaching the Gospel; let him be anathema [accursed, damned] (*Dogmatic Canons & Decrees of the Council of Trent;* Devin-Adair Co.).

There are 15 Canons that relate to penance, but we will end with a few thoughts as related to Canon III.

Penance appears to be the "all powerful" sacrament. It includes confession and the absolution of sin. It is through this sacrament that the Roman Church answers yes, most powerfully, to the question: Is man God?

In making the point that the hierarchy of the Roman Church is a "grand fact" in history – a fact so important that there would be no history without it," the author, Michael Muller, C.S.S.R., states that "the Pope, the bishops and priests are the light of the world, the salt of the earth, the mediators between God and man" (*The Catholic Priest,* Kreuzer Brothers, Baltimore, Page 15-16).

The priests are mediators between God and man? Here is what the Bible has to say about who is our mediatior; it is Christ and Christ alone!!

> And for this cause he is the mediator of a new covenant, that a death having taken place for the redemption of the transgressions that were under the first covenant (Hebrews 9:15 ASV).
>
> And so fearful was the appearance, that Moses said, I exceedingly fear and quake: but ye are come unto mount Zion, and unto the city of the living God, the heavenly Jerusalem, and to innumerable hosts of angels, to the general assembly and church of the firstborn who are enrolled in heaven, and to God the Judge of all, and to the spirits of just men made perfect, and to Jesus the mediator of a new covenant, and to the blood of sprinkling that speaketh better than *that of* Abel (Hebrews 12:21-24 ASV).
>
> For every high priest, being taken from among men, is appointed for men in things pertaining to God, that he may offer both gifts and sacrifices for sins – So Christ also glorified not himself to be made a high priest, but he that spake unto him, Thou art my Son, This day have I begotten thee (Hebrews 5:1, 5 ASV).

To claim that the hierarchy of the Roman Church is the mediator between God and man is to accuse God of being a liar. First Peter 2 states that our "sacrifices" are offered to God through Jesus Christ. Christ is our High Priest forever. The living stones (believers) in the church are described as "holy priesthood." There is no mediator between the believer and Christ and He is our only mediator. The thought of the Roman priest being mediators between God and man is abominable.

The authority the Roman Church proclaims for this ability is three-fold.

> And I also say unto thee, that thou art Peter, and upon this rock I will build my church; and the gates of Hades shall not prevail against it. I will give unto thee the keys of the kingdom of heaven: and whatsoever thou shalt bind on earth shall be bound in heaven; and whatsoever thou shalt loose on earth shall be loosed in heaven (Matthew 16:18-19 ASV).
>
> Verily I say unto you, what things soever ye shall bind on earth shall be bound in heaven; and what things soever ye shall loose on earth shall be loosed in heaven. Again I say unto you, that if two of you shall agree on earth as touching anything that they shall ask, it shall be done for them of my Father who is in heaven (Matthew 18:18-19 ASV).
>
> And when he had said this, he breathed on them, and saith unto them, Receive ye the Holy Spirit: whose soever sins ye forgive, they are forgiven unto them; whose soever sins ye retain, they are retained (John 20:22-23 ASV).

Consider again Numbers 23:19 (ASV):
> God is not a man, that he should lie, Neither the son of man, that he should repent: Hath he said, and will he not do it? Or hath he spoken, and will he not make it good?

Repeatedly, over and over again, God, in the Bible, has stated that salvation is by faith, that it is permanent, and that all our sins (past, present, and future) are forgiven in Christ's finished work on the cross. Considering this, and the fact that God cannot lie, then what is not being talked about in these three passages is the power of the Catholic hierarchy to forgive and retain sins in a way to either admit one to heaven or bar one from it. But this is exactly what the Roman Church claims. Is man God?

Keep in mind that the conversation in Matthew 16:18 begins with Christ's question in verse 16:13 by asking His disciples "Who do men say that I, the Son of Man, am?" Peter gives the right answer; it is his "confession" of faith in Christ. In this section Christ points out that Peter means "little rock" (in Greek also of masculine gender) and thereby compares him with his "confession," which Christ calls a large stone or rock (in the Greek language of feminine gender).

The church, said Christ, will be built upon that confession. That said, one will need to understand that the "binding and loosing" will have to be in accord with the Chief Cornerstone's guidance. The binding and loosing was given only to the Apostles. As we will see, there is NO apostolic succession, so the "keys" or the power of binding and loosing no longer exists in the hands of men. This will be discussed in depth later.

The Chief Cornerstone is Christ. He is in moment-by-moment control of His Body, the Church. Since He is the Word of God, one will know that all binding and loosing will not conflict with Scripture.

Following are some more astonishing statements from Mr. Muller.
> Transubstantiation [he is speaking of the Eucharist/Mass] —the New Incarnation—which is but an extension of the first. And what Mary did

once, the priest does every day. While she gave to the Son of God a life of suffering, which ended by the torment of the cross, the priest renders Him present, in his hands, in a state immortal and impassible.

It is in establishing the priesthood that God seems to have exhausted all the treasures of His power and mercy. Indeed, in light of faith, the man disappears altogether in the priest. Faith beholds in him nothing but Jesus Christ. [The Priest is transubstantiated into Christ!]

Faith sees but Jesus Christ in the priest when he remits sin.

Faith sees but Jesus Christ in the priest when he consecrates at Mass; for at the consecration the priest does not say: This is Christ's body; he says; **this is MY body** (*The Catholic Priest* by Michael Muller, C.S.S.R.; Kreuzer Brothers, Baltimore, pp. 106-107).

Only God can remit sin and absolve man of his guilt. As we see, though, the Roman Church believes, as demonstrated by its practices, that the answer is yes to the question: Is man God? Why do I say this? Read Michael Muller's comments again. The Roman Church's position is that the priest becomes God in these "magical" ceremonies.

Sacrament of Confirmation

What is Confirmation? It is one of the three sacraments of initiation. The other two are baptism and the eucharist. Why are they called the sacraments of initiation? Because they are the sacraments to be "received by a person, whereby their relationship and connection to the Church is fully established." —Membership has its privileges, as well as duties and obligations. Fully initiated members are expected to come to Mass every weekend and to go to confession (*The Catholicism Answer Book;* Rev. John Trigilio, Jr., PHD, THD and Rev. Kenneth Brighenti, PHD, Page 109).

Salvation is not involved in the confirmation ceremony, but it is stated that "grace" is imparted to the catechumen. It is the grace of "full maturity." It claimed that it brings sanctification to the catechumen.

> In order to be confirmed, the catechumen must first have been baptized, received first penance, and First Holy Communion (ibid. p. 106).

The sacrament is executed on those between the ages of seven and sixteen. It is administered by the Bishop, by laying on of hands, application of the "Chrism" (anointing oil) and the somewhat magic appearing actions and words as follows:

> "I sign thee with the sign of the cross, and confirm thee with the chrism of salvation, in the name of the Father, and of the Son, and of the Holy Ghost"... (at the end of this ritual, the person) "begins to be settled in firmness by the strength of a new virtue, and thus to become a perfect soldier of Christ" (For full detail refer to *The Catechism of the Council of Trent,* B.A. Buckley, pp. 196-209).

"Confirm thee with the chrism of salvation?" Just where is this in the Bible? The "chrism," by the way, is "oil." One wonders if it has to be of a certain weight, like 30 weight, or 10/30 all seasons oil?

> The function of this sacrament is teaching the Catechumen about the seven gifts of the Holy Spirit, imparted to him/her at Baptism. These gifts are Wisdom (natural world common sense,) Understanding (helps

in the supernatural world to understand faith and morals,) Knowledge (helps to understand and do God's will,) Piety (outlook on life, prepares the catechumen for eternity with God,) Fear of the Lord (a gift of holy reverence to revere God.... These gifts of the Holy Spirit give us a discerning spirit (*The Catholicism Answer Book;* Rev. John Trigilio, Jr., PHD, THD and Rev. Kenneth Brighenti, PHD, Page 108).

Canon 1: If anyone says that the confirmation of those who have been baptized is an idle ceremony, and not rather a true and proper sacrament; or that of old it was nothing more than a kind of catechism whereby they who were near adolescence gave an account of their faith in the face of the church; let him be anathema [accursed, damned].

Canon 2: If anyone says that they who ascribe any virtue to the sacred chrism of the confirmation of an outrage to the Holy Ghost; let him be anathema [accursed, damned].

Canon 3: If anyone says that the ordinary minister of holy confirmation is not the bishop alone, but any simple priest so ever; let him be anathema [accursed, damned].

(*Dogmatic Canons & Decrees, Council of Trent,* Devin-Adair Co., Page 66)

In these Canons, the Roman Church is threatening all with damnation for something that is not in the Bible. You can search fore and aft in the Bible and not find anything related to a ritual called confirmation. In the *Catechism of Trent* it is claimed in one spot that this was ordained by Peter and in another, by Christ. But, there is no reference to either as having established this vain ritual in the Bible. Further, there is nothing in the Bible about the seven-fold gifts of the Holy Spirit.

In short, confirmation is no more efficacious than going through an initiation ceremony for a fraternity or sorority. Further, rather than through it having received wisdom, understanding and a discerning spirit, more hocus pocus and superstition is imparted to the communicant.

Extreme Unction

What is extreme unction? Today we know it more commonly as the last rites. The amazing thing about this ritual is that it did not become a ritual until the twelfth century (1100s A.D.). This is something that was added to the Roman Church's liturgy right out of the mysticism of the age. It is man saying yes to the question: "Is man God?"

Ostensibly, this ritual is based upon this Bible passage:

> Is any among you suffering? Let him pray. Is any cheerful? Let him sing praise. Is any among you sick? Let him call for the elders of the church; and let them pray over him, anointing him with oil in the name of the Lord: and the prayer of faith shall save him that is sick, and the Lord shall raise him up; and if he have committed sins, it shall be forgiven him (James 5:13-15 ASV).

What is the intended meaning of this passage? It refers to being raised up by the Lord and sins forgiven. Is the restoration to sound health referred to, preparation for death, or both? Whichever it is, the elders are to be called for.

The Greek word for elder here is *presbuteros* or presbyter in English. It is translated through the Bible as elder – except in some Catholic Bibles. In the *Douay-Rheims Bible*, it is translated Priest, which is an untruth. The Greek word for Priest is "hierus." In the newer *Catholic Study Bible* the translation is to the word presbyter.

In the *Trent Catechism*, they also use the word presbyter, but define the meaning as priest:

> For it is there (James 5:13-15) shown that the proper ministers of this sacrament are the presbyters of the Church (canon iv); by which name are to be understood, in that place, not the elders by age, or the foremost in dignity amongst the people, but either bishops, or priests by bishops rightly ordained by the imposition of the hands of the priesthood (canon iv) (*Dogmatic Canons & Decrees, Council of Trent.* Devin-Adair Co., pp. 117-118).

The term "elders" was used to define the members of the

Sanhedrin, the 70 Jewish leaders that looked after the welfare of Israel. This group included some priests, but also people of other callings, such as the scribes, which were lawyers. In the body of Christ, the Church, the elders are the leaders of the local church. There is no function for the priesthood, as practiced by the Roman Church.

In the book *Catechism of Trent* by B.A. Buckley, beginning on page 302, this section starts out with a quote, ostensibly from either Ecclesiastes or Ecclesiasticus 7:40. The words claimed by the Fathers at Trent are these:

> In all thy works, say the oracles of Holy Scripture, remember thy last end, and thou will not sin.

It is a nice thought, but no one except Christ has ever "not sinned." Can you believe there is no verse 7:40 in either of the Books cited? Someone, at Trent, either made this up or inserted the wrong reference. I cannot find a corresponding reference in my computer Bibles, so I am going with the made-up conclusion. Most of what came out of Trent was made up. The material is grimmer than *Grimm's Fairy Tales.*

Buckley's comment, however, does set the scene for what the Roman Church sees as the need for this ritual. Man is unable to view his last end and use that view as a motivation to live righteously. Man is a sinner and will die that way unless something is done. The question is this, what is it that needs to be done?

Extreme unction needs to be applied at the point of death insists the Roman Church. Here is how the Roman Church explains extreme unction. This is from the introductory remarks in the *Catholic Encyclopedia:*

> A sacrament of the New Law instituted by Christ to give spiritual aid and comfort and perfect spiritual health, including, if need be, the remission of sins, and also, conditionally, to restore bodily health, to Christians who are seriously ill; it consists essentially in the unction by a priest of the body of the sick person, **accompanied by a suitable form of words** (http://www.newadvent.org/cathen/05716a.htm).

A suitable form of words? This makes me think of magical terms like abracadabra, or openseseme! Let's look at more of the encyclopedia's treasury of knowledge.

ESCAPE FROM PAGANISM

> As administered in the Western Church today according to the rite of the Roman Ritual, the sacrament consists **(apart from certain non-essential prayers)** in the unction with oil, specially blessed by the bishop, of the organs of the five external senses (eyes, ears, nostrils, lips, hands), of the feet, and, for men (where the custom exists and the condition of the patient permits of his being moved), of the loins or reins; and in the following form repeated at each unction with mention of the corresponding sense or faculty: 'Through this holy unction and His own most tender mercy may the Lord pardon thee whatever sins or faults thou hast committed [quidquid deliquisti] by sight [by hearing, smell, taste, touch, walking, carnal delectation].' The unction of the loins is generally, if not universally, omitted in English-speaking countries, and it is of course everywhere forbidden in case of women (ibid).

This passage needs some consideration, especially in light of the instructions they claim from the Book of James.

- Non-essential prayer? Look at the James passage again. Prayer seems to be at the heart of the issue.
- Sacrament consists . . . in the unction with oil, specially blessed by the bishop, of the organs of the five external senses (eyes, ears, nostrils, lips, hands and feet) and, for men (where the custom exists and the condition of the patient permits of his being moved), of the loins or reins (*Extreme Unction,* Catholic Encyclopedia, Page 1).

"Call for the elders of the church; and let them pray over him." Where does this idea of "non-essential prayer come from? Actually, we have seen above with this ritual, **prayer is unnecessary** – well, that is what they say by their description of the efficacy of this ritual.

The oil is applied to the five external senses–actually six when you add in the groin area described as the "loins or reins." It is as if these sensors were the source of sin. This is confirmed on another Roman Church website.

> Through this holy unction and His own most tender mercy may the Lord pardon thee whatever sins or faults thou hast committed [quidquid deliquisti] by sight, by hearing, smell, taste, touch, walking, carnal delectation (http://www.catholic.org/encyclopedia/view.php?id=11802).

This is sorcery at work. Sin is not the product of our senses or organs. It is the product of our being. To be cleansed of sin we must be born again through belief in the Lord Jesus as our Savior and Lord. Having a little oil rubbed here and there over our body is not going to do anything for us, other than make us greasy!

According to the Roman Church, though:

> Here we have the physical elements necessary to constitute a sacrament in the strict sense: oil as remote matter, like water in baptism; the anointing as proximate matter, like immersion or infusion in baptism; and the accompanying prayer as form. This rite will therefore be a true sacrament if it has the sanction of Christ's authority, and is intended by its own operation to confer grace on the sick person, to work for his spiritual benefit (http://www.newadvent.org/cathen/05716a.htm).

Even the analysis of the person's "scribbling" that wrote this article for the *Catholic Encyclopedia* does not come close in establishing that this ritual has the sanction of Christ. How could it? It contravenes all that the Bible has to say about forgiveness of sin and the obtaining of salvation.

This phrase is interesting to note. What it says is a general statement for each of the sacraments: "and is intended by its own operation to confer grace on the sick person."

Now think about this: intended by **its own** operation! This is like a robotic lawn mower. Program it, turn it on, and go have lunch while it mows your lawn. This phrase describes the belief that is lodged in all the sacraments: whatever they do, they do mechanically, or rather "magically." A good analogy would be the genie in the bottle. Whatever the sacrament does, it is intrinsic to itself. It needs no outside input from God, but only the conduct of the ritual by the Priest or Bishop.

Further, nothing is really required of the communicant except, in this case, **to get oiled.** The person can be unconscious, but the sacrament intercedes for him or her. All it takes are some "appropriate words," some olive oil, and some rubs on the right spots for this ritual to be effective. This is sorcery for sure. Est homo Deus? (Is man God?) With all these magical sacraments at man's disposal, don't you suppose that the answer would be yes? But only if they worked, right?

They do not work. The poor person that relies on extreme unction or any of the sacraments for salvation only winds up in hell for eternity. Pope Benedict is wrong about the Roman Church being the only path to eternal life. The path the Roman Church charts is to that other place.

What was James referring to when he wrote about calling the elders in for prayer over the sick person? One would have to say that healing an illness through the prayers of the Elders of the Church constitutes a miracle. However, it is theologically dangerous to base any "theological" truth on a couple of verses. So, let's add some.

> Take, brethren, for an example of suffering and of patience, the prophets who spake in the name of the Lord. Behold, we call them blessed that endured: ye have heard of the patience of Job, and have seen the end of the Lord, how that the Lord is full of pity, and merciful (James 5:10-11 ASV).

> Is any among you suffering? Let him pray. Is any cheerful? Let him sing praise. Is any among you sick? Let him call for the elders of the church; and let them pray over him, anointing him with oil in the name of the Lord: and the prayer of faith shall save him that is sick, and the Lord shall raise him up; and if he have committed sins, it shall be forgiven him. Confess therefore your sins one to another, and pray one for another, that ye may be healed. The supplication of a righteous man availeth much in its working. Elijah was a man of like passions with us, and he prayed fervently that it might not rain; and it rained not on the earth for three years and six months. And he prayed again; and the heaven gave rain, and the earth brought forth her fruit (James 5:13-18 ASV).

This section talks about suffering and endurance. We are admonished to consider:

- The prophets (verse 10).
- Job (verse 11).
- And reminded of Elijah, a prophet (verse 17).

Where are these people? They are all absent from the body and present with the Lord, today. It is like the statement by the famous evangelist Dwight L. Moody: "One day you will read in a newspaper that I have died. Don't believe it, because at that moment I will be more alive than you!"

Absent from the body, may not be the description of Elijah's present condition for the Lord took him to heaven on a chariot in a whirlwind of fire. The fact is, though, that the Lord "raised him up."

> And it came to pass, as they still went on, and talked, that, behold, there appeared a chariot of fire, and horses of fire, which parted them both asunder; and Elijah went up by a whirlwind into heaven (2 Kings 2:11 ASV).

What about Job and the other prophets. We know the suffering and triumph of Job and how he lost all that he had including his health. We know this loss was the direct result of Satan being allowed by God to attack Job. Satan's intent was to show God that His children would be unfaithful to Him if they were put through suffering and trials. Satan lost.

Where is Job today?

> But as for me I know that my Redeemer liveth, And at last he will stand up upon the earth: And after my skin, even this body, is destroyed, Then without my flesh shall I see God; Whom I, even I, shall see, on my side, And mine eyes shall behold, and not as a stranger. My heart is consumed within me (Job 19:25-27 ASV).

Consider, then, the rest of the prophets:

> Others were tortured, not accepting their deliverance; that they might obtain a better resurrection: and others had trial of mockings and scourgings, yea, moreover of bonds and imprisonment: they were stoned, they were sawn asunder, they were tempted, they were slain with the sword: they went about in sheepskins, in goatskins; being destitute, afflicted, ill-treated (of whom the world was not worthy), wandering in deserts and mountains and caves, and the holes of the earth (Hebrews 11:32-38 ASV).

These, too, were raised up by the Lord and are present with Him in heaven today. We have Christ's direct testimony to this.

> I am the God of Abraham, and the God of Isaac, and the God of Jacob. God is not the God of the dead, but of the living (Matthew 22:32 ASV).

Here Christ states that Abraham, Isaac, and Jacob are among the living. They are not among the living on earth. They are among the living in heaven. This applies to the other prophets also. All of these people endured to the end. The passage from James says that "we call them blessed that endured." Since there are only two possibilities for an eternal destiny, heaven or hell, you would have to say the destiny of the prophets was heaven as they are "blessed."

As to this passage there is an important clue here. The prayers of the elders may or may not result in the sick person getting physically well. This person may, in the natural sense, die. The clue is how the word "raised" is intended.

There are two possibilities for this person:
- The Lord decides to "heal" the person physically and "raises" him up.
- The Lord determines the days of the sick person are over and allows him to die, physically. If this person is a believer, then the Lord "raises" him up also. He raises him up into heaven.

The word "raise" is used eleven times in the New Testament in reference to "raising the dead." It is never used for "healing" the sick. With this in mind, consider that "prayer of faith" that James refers to:

> And the prayer of faith shall save him that is sick, and the Lord shall raise him up; and if he have committed sins, it shall be forgiven him (James 5:15 (ASV).

I am not saying that this cannot also refer to restoring the sick to physical health. That person will eventually die physically. Remember Lazarus? Jesus raised him from the dead, but do you see Lazarus walking around on the earth today? No, at some point he died physically.

It can refer to restoration of health, but it more strongly refers to raising the believer to heaven to begin an eternity in the presence of the Lord. In either case, the prayer of "faith" is important. It is the "key" to the person's eternal destiny. It is the prayer for salvation. It is this person's expression of faith in Christ Jesus as his Lord, his Savior. James is talking about the sick person coming to newness of life, being "born again."

Again, it is "sola fidae" (salvation only by faith) as the reformers stated and which the Bible teaches.

Eucharist Mass

It is the day of the Passover. We have followed a macabre parade from Pontius Pilate's residence, down the road to Golgotha. There we watch the Roman soldiers nail Jesus Christ to the cross and drop it into the post hole prepared for it. As the ninth hour appears:

> After this Jesus, knowing that all things are now finished, that the scripture might be accomplished, saith, I thirst. There was set there a vessel full of vinegar: so they put a sponge full of the vinegar upon hyssop, and brought it to his mouth. When Jesus therefore had received the vinegar, he said, It is finished: and he bowed his head, and gave up his spirit (John 19:28-30 ASV).

"It is finished," said Jesus.

Wait, it is **not** finished! Jesus, don't you know that there will be an organization in 300 years that will claim to kill you daily for each communicant participating in a ritual that they will call the Eucharist/Mass? This ritual will be performed twice each day. You are to be sacrificed billions of times. Further, it will be done by priests who say that they are transformed into You each time they prepare the bread and wine for this ritual. I guess they are trying to make it look like suicide, but it is **mass murder** for real.

They deceive themselves, do they not? They are twisting Scriptures to their own destruction and to the destruction of their flocks. What a horrible charade.

Yes, what the Roman Catholic Church does not realize is that when Christ said, "It is finished," it really was finished.

What was finished? The sacrifice for sin was finished. The Scriptures have much to say about it. It would be good to read the Letter to the Hebrews at this point. See for yourself what God has to say about "It is finished."

God made Christ "perfect" through His suffering.

> It became him, for whom are all things, and through whom are all things, in bringing many sons unto glory, to make the author of their salvation perfect through sufferings (Hebrews 2:10 ASV).

God made Him perfect for what?

> Since then the children are sharers in flesh and blood, he also himself in like manner partook of the same; that through death he might bring to nought him that had the power of death, that is, the devil; and might deliver all them who through fear of death were all their lifetime subject to bondage. For verily not to angels doth he give help, but he giveth help to the seed of Abraham. Wherefore it behooved him in all things to be made like unto his brethren, that he might become a merciful and faithful high priest in things pertaining to God, to make propitiation for the sins of the people. For in that he himself hath suffered being tempted, he is able to succor them that are tempted (Hebrews 2:14-18 ASV).

There is a lot said in this little bit of Scripture:

- Christ needed to share in flesh and blood.
- His death would destroy the devil (he had the power of death).
- He freed those enslaved to the fear of death.
- Christ became fully human (but still fully God) to be our High Priest.
- As our High Priest, He made propitiation for our sins (note: the word propitiation is singular, not plural: one propitiation, not many).

What does the word "propitiation" mean? Its meaning is to appease. In context it is to appease God concerning our sins, and to reconcile us to Him.

> And they indeed have been made priests many in number, because that by death they are hindered from continuing: but he, because he abideth for ever, hath his priesthood unchangeable. Wherefore also he is able to save to the uttermost them that draw near unto God through him, seeing he ever liveth to make intercession for them. For such a high priest became us, holy, guileless, undefiled, separated from sinners, and made higher than the heavens; who needeth not daily, like those high priests, to offer up sacrifices, first for his own sins, and then for the sins of the people: for this he did once for all, when he offered up himself. For the law appointeth men high priests, having infirmity;

but the word of the oath, which was after the law, appointeth a Son, perfected for evermore (Hebrews 7:23-28 ASV).

God required appeasement for man's sin; man needed reconciliation to God. Since the wages of sin is death, man could appease God with his own death, but then he could not be reconciled, as he would be dead. Christ, our High Priest, offered Himself as the sacrifice for the sins of the world. He died upon that cross. However, He was perfect and without sin. He conquered death and the one that had the power of death, the devil. Jesus' sacrifice appeased God and reconciled man to God, that through faith in Jesus, man would have eternal life. Notice, only one offering by Christ was needed. When He looked down from that cross and said that it was finished, it was finished. This was and is **the only solution for sin.**

Christ's one death and one resurrection, provides the **one way** to eternal life for all who put their faith in Him. It is eternal life that commences upon belief and never lapses, skips a beat, takes a vacation, or is interrupted by subsequent sin. How can this be?

> Wherefore when he cometh into the world, he saith, Sacrifice and offering thou wouldest not, But a body didst thou prepare for me; In whole burnt offerings and *sacrifices* for sin thou hadst no pleasure: Then said I, Lo, I am come (In the roll of the book it is written of me) To do thy will, O God. Saying above, Sacrifices and offerings and whole burnt offerings and *sacrifices* for sin thou wouldest not, neither hadst pleasure therein (the which are offered according to the law), then hath he said, Lo, I am come to do thy will. He taketh away the first, that he may establish the second. By which will we have been sanctified through the offering of the body of Jesus Christ once for all. And every priest indeed standeth day by day ministering and offering oftentimes the same sacrifices, the which can never take away sins: but he, when he had offered one sacrifice for sins for ever, sat down on the right hand of God; henceforth expecting till his enemies be made the footstool of his feet. For by one offering he hath perfected for ever them that are sanctified. And the Holy Spirit also beareth witness to us; for after he hath said, This is the covenant that I will make with them After those days, saith the Lord: I will put my laws on their heart, And upon their mind also will I write them; *then saith he,* And their sins and their iniquities will I remember no more. Now where remission of these is, there is no more offering for sin (Hebrews 10:5-18 ASV).

The Roman Church has perverted the Gospel. Christ's one offering was not adequate they say. Christ has to be killed over and over and over again. For them there is no solution for sin.

What immediately follows is from *Dogmatic Canons and Decrees of The Council of Trent,* The Devin-Adair Company, New York, 1912. This book carries the Imprimatur of John Cardinal Farley, Archbishop of New York, and the NobilObstat of Remigius Lafort, D.D. Censor.

> The purposes of the Eucharist are these:
> - To provide a symbol so that all Christians might be united.
> - To remember His wonderful works.
> - To venerate His [Christ's] memory.
> - To provide spiritual food for the soul.
> - To provide sanctification.
> - To provide a sacrifice for sin [this part is the Mass].
>
> There are three classes of people who receive the Eucharist
> - Sinners receiving it as a sacrament.
> - Others receiving it spiritually.
> - Those that receive it both ways.

The Mass is the "sacrifice" part of the eucharist.

The Council of Trent considered this issue twice. The results of their deliberations were presented first as the "Most Holy Sacrament of the Eucharist" and second as the "Sacrifice of the Mass."

> The Eucharist, that true bread from heaven that nourishes our souls to eternal life (*Catechism,* page 107).
>
> The Eucharist is the pre-eminent Sacrament because it is the one that which the communicant is "directly united to God" (*Catechism,* page 80).

How is this accomplished? It is claimed that the elements become the body and blood of the Redeemer. That wafer or bread that is put in your mouth is actually, physically, really the body and blood of Christ. What about the wine that the priest drinks? It, too, is supposed to be the actual body and blood of the Lord Jesus Christ.

From pages 173 to 175, *Catechism* has this to say:

> ...the Eucharist was instituted by our Lord for two great purposes, to be the celestial food of the soul, preserving and supporting spiritual life, and to give to the Church a **perpetual sacrifice,** by which sin may be expiated, and our heavenly Father, whom our crimes have often grievously offended, may be turned from wrath to mercy...

> ...the paschal lamb, which was offered and eaten by the Israelites as a sacrament and sacrifice, was a lively figure. Nor could our divine Lord, when about to offer himself to his eternal Father on the altar of the cross, have given a more illustrious proof of his unbounded love for us, than by bequeathing to us a visible sacrifice, by which the boldly sacrifice ... was to be offered once on the cross, was to be renewed and its memory celebrated daily throughout the universal Church ...

The Eucharist is both a sacrament and a sacrifice.

> As a sacrament, it is also to the worthy receiver a source of merit.... as a sacrifice it is not only a source of merit, but also of satisfaction.... in the oblation of this sacrifice, which is a bond of Christian unity, Christians merit the fruit of his passion and satisfy for sin.

It is clear that each time you participate in the eucharist you are participating in a sacrament through which you gain merit. That merit is applied to the simultaneous sacrifice of the mass. The sacrament involves eating the physical and entire Lord Jesus. The sacrifice is the killing of the Lord Jesus again for the sins you have committed since your baptism or the last eucharist/mass you attended.

One other observation gleaned from *Catechism,* page 175:

> The words of consecration declare: The priest is also the same, Christ our Lord: the ministers, who offer this sacrifice, consecrate the holy mysteries not in their own but in the person of Christ.

That's right, the priest ceases being himself and he, too, in addition to the elements, becomes Jesus Christ in the flesh. Est homo Deus? (Is man God?) Again, the Roman Church says yes.

We need to comment here about just a few points. This is a false and repugnant ritual!

- First, the claim that this sacrament ***provides a symbol so that all Christians might be unified:***

    All Christians are unified. A Christian is defined as one who has placed his/her faith in their Lord and Savior, Jesus Christ, and Him alone. They are trusting only in His finished work for their salvation, no rituals, prayers to Mary or the saints, no merit of their own, but in Christ alone. As such they have been born from above, a new creation, united to the body of Christ, His Church, by the Holy Spirit. Unity is a fact without a symbol. If you are not unified to Christ through faith, you are not a Christian.

- ***To provide sanctification.***

    You cannot be sanctified through a magical or mechanical ritual such as the eucharist/mass. This is hocus-pocus, abracadabra stuff. The term sanctification means "to be set apart for the Lord and changed into His character by the indwelling Holy Spirit."

- ***To provide sacrifice for sin and to be a perpetual sacrifice.***

    Read the passages from Hebrews again. Christ is our one sacrifice. On the cross, He said that it was finished. God was appeased and Christ was given all rule, power and authority. He sat down at the right hand of God where He intercedes for us. To say that we need a perpetual sacrifice for our sins, is to make the Triune God a liar. Shudder, yes, shudder, when you think of calling God a liar. The Roman Church has been doing it for the last 1700 years on this issue alone. The leadership (popes to priests) is awaiting the second death and an eternity in the Lake of Fire for this issue alone.

- ***To provide a "worthy" receiver, a source of merit.***

    One should "retch" over this. God says in His Word "There are none righteous, no not one" (Romans 3:10). "All have become worthless (Romans 3:12). "All have fallen short of the glory of God" (Romans 3:23). Merit is the reward for something that you do. It is compensation for a work. God has this to say about our works: "for by grace have ye been saved through faith; and that not of yourselves, it is the gift of God; not of works, that no man should glory" (Ephesians 2:8-9).

The eucharist/mass is a foul, evil ritual, and devoid of any salvific connection with the God of Heaven. In fact, it and all the other sacraments work to make God a liar.

The Canons of Trent related to the eucharist/mass include these:

> **Canon 1**: If anyone saith that in the Mass a true and proper sacrifice is not offered to God; or that to be offered is nothing else but that Christ is given us to eat; let him be anathema.
>
> **Canon 2:** If anyone saith that by these words, "Do this for the commemoration of Me," Christ did not institute the Apostles priests; or did not ordain that they and other priests should offer His own body and blood; let him be anathema.
>
> **Canon 4:** If anyone saith that, by the sacrifice of the Mass, a blasphemy is cast upon the most holy sacrifice of Christ consummated on the Cross; or that it is thereby derogated from; let him be anathema.

It is time to restate what is included in the term "anathema." Its meaning includes being accursed and damned. The Word of God, the Bible, clearly disagrees with the Canons documented in this chapter. Since the Word of God originates with God, then by the definition of these Canons, the Roman Church has damned God. Est homo Deus? Again the Roman Church says yes, it thinks man is God.

The Wafer God

> And as they were eating, Jesus took bread, and blessed, and brake it; and he gave to the disciples, and said, Take, eat; this is my body. And he took a cup, and gave thanks, and gave to them, saying, Drink ye all of it; for this is my blood of the covenant, which is poured out for many unto remission of sins. But I say unto you, I shall not drink henceforth of this fruit of the vine, until that day when I drink it new with you in my Father's kingdom (Matt 26:26 ASV).

I start here with the "wafer god" for the purpose of demonstrating the shape of the bread that Jesus distributed to the disciples. This bread was "Passover" bread. That is, it was unleavened. Notice that Jesus "broke" the bread. You can purchase this type of bread at most grocery stores. If you do, and you want to divide it up with others, no doubt you will break it into pieces. Each piece will be irregularly shaped and sized.

The wafer distributed at the eucharist/mass, is not so. It is a precisely round wafer. Each wafer is the same size and shape. It **must** be so, as this is the dictate of the Roman Church. Does it have any special significance? I think so. It is directly out of paganism.

The pagans worshipped the sun, among other deities. The name of this god for the Egyptians was Osiris. Somehow, Osiris, became the son of the Queen of Heaven (Isis). As this son, his name was He-Siri, which means corn, or seed. From the time of Adam and Eve, people knew of the coming Seed. Those that hoped for the real Seed, or the head crusher of Satan, had faith in the Living God, the Creator of all.

From Cain and his descendants, devotees of man made-religion, throughout the years, this Osiris/Isis/He-Siri Satanic fraud was developed. Its origin after Noah's flood was Babylon. It spread throughout the whole world from this beginning.

Consider the embellishments of the Roman altar to their equivalent of Osiris.

> A plate of silver, in the form of a Sun, is fixed opposite to the sacrament on the altar; which, with the light of the tapers, makes a most brilliant Appearance (*The Two Babylons* by Alexander Hislop, Page 162).

What has that brilliant sun to do there, on the altar, over against the sacrament or round wafer? This representation, incidentally, is the same in ancient Egypt, Rome, Babylon, and would you believe it, Cuzco, Peru! The round wafer, in the Roman Church, represents their god, as did the sacrament in the old pagan religions. It has its derivation from the pagan worship of the sun. All the "faithful" worshiped the image or idol of the sun. The wafer was adored (worshipped) as God.

In the Roman Church the round wafer is displayed in the "monstrance." What is a "monstrance?" It is the symbol of the sun with rays shooting out from it. The wafer is in the center of the rays and is representative of the sun or Osiris. The monstrance is a copy of the plate of silver used on the altars of Egypt. You can read more about this disgusting worship of heathen gods in the book, *The Two Babylons* by Rev. Alexander Hislop, or "Google" it online. You can type in "monstrance" or "wafer god" and get an abundance of information.

This monstrance is an idol and is worshipped. The wafer in the center is the wafer god. The monstrance is a monster of demonic development.

The mass/eucharist is not something started by Christ, but started way before His incarnation. It is the outgrowth of what Cain knew about the coming seed (Christ). He and his descendents created (with satanic guidance) a false religious system in rebellion to the living God. This is called paganism. The Roman Church has continued it. Their adoration (worship) of the wafer is the wafer god of old.

Cannibalism?

Escape From Paganism

The doctrine of Transubstantiation is that the elements (bread and wine) of the eucharist/mass are actually the entire body of our Lord Jesus Christ. Think of it, flesh, bone, hide, hair, blood, guts and gore; it is all there according to the Roman Church catechism. If this is so, isn't the communicant (the person receiving the elements and eating them) a cannibal?

Believe it or not, this issue was debated by the "intellectuals" of the Roman Church back in the 12th, 13th and later centuries. A whole series of "miracles" (lying wonders) were fabricated to prove the real presence of Christ in the wafer. The wafer would bleed, would not burn, was reverenced and worshipped by animals and insects and many other "true" fairy tales.

One example was that a matron had secreted a wafer out of the church and put it in her beehive to protect the bees and cause them to flourish. The bees were so humbled that they built a chapel out of wax, complete with windows, spire, and bell, and placed the wafer within. The parish priest came to witness this and the news was spread throughout the Roman Church.

Catholic writers had a time explaining the issue of cannibalism.

> Thomas Aimon stated: "the taste and figure of bread and wine as remaining in the sacrament, to prevent the horror of the communicant."
>
> Lanfranc stated: "the species remain, lest the spectator should be horrified at the sight of the raw and bloody flesh."
>
> Hugo acknowledged that "few would approach the communion, if blood should appear in the cup, and the flesh should appear red as in the shambles."
>
> Durand admits that "human infirmity, unaccustomed to eat man's flesh, would, if the substance were seen, refuse participation."
>
> Aquinas avows "the horror of swallowing human flesh and blood."

"The smell, the species, and the taste of bread and wine remain," says the sainted Bernard, "to conceal flesh and blood, which, if offered without disguise as meat and drink, might horrify human weakness."

(Quotes from *The History of Romanism* by J.J. Dowling D. D., pages 201-202.)

Even the Roman Church intellectuals recognize the transubstantiation, and the eucharist/mass as cannibalism.

Is this not revolting?

Dung!

Have you ever heard of the issue of "Stercorianism?" As related to transubstantiation it was as big an issue as cannibalism. What is Stercorianism? The root of the word is Stercus which, when translated into English, means dung!

How does this fit into the issue of transubstantiation? Eating of the elements raises the issue of what happens to them once they are consumed. Are they excreted and become part of the dung heap?

> One Roman Church "intellectual," Paschasius, maintained "that bread and wine in the sacrament are not under the same laws with our other food, as they pass into our flesh and substance without any evacuation" *(History of Romanism,* Dowley page 195).

When we think about it, and the number of times one might take mass in their lifetime, we have to wonder how many Christs are part of their body.

To answer this question, the learned fathers said that the elements were annihilated. Woops! Did not the priest create God, the creator, in the elements? Annihalated? That means that God is destroyed. It has to. If the wafer **is** the God/Man, Christ, and it is annihilated, then God has been destroyed. This is nonsense, but then the whole issue of transubstantiation is nonsense.

I think it is clear, that the wafer is digested and excreted the way that other food is. If the elements were really Christ; hide, hair, blood, guts and gore, then this would transform our Lord Christ, our sacrifice without spot or wrinkle, into filth. According to transubstantiation, Jesus becomes dung!

This is abhorrent, repugnant, retching, and a lie. Fortunately it is also make believe and has nothing to do with Christianity. It is just another proof of the Roman Church's paganism.

Sacrament of Orders

This is how the Rev. J. Waterworth introduces the sacrament of orders in his book *The Sacred and Oecumenical Council of Trent* (The Catholic Publication Society, 1848):

> Whereas, by the testimony of Scripture, by the Apostolic tradition, and the unanimous consent of the Fathers, it is clear that grace is conferred the sacred ordination, which is performed by the words and outward signs, no one ought to doubt that Order is truly and properly one of the seven sacraments of the holy Church. For the Apostle says: "admonish thee that thou stir up the grace of God, which is in thee by the imposition of my hands. For God has not given us the spirit of fear, but of power, and of love and of sobriety" (2 Timothy 1:6-7).

Keep in mind that the Council of Trent was reaffirmed by Vatican II, and the current Pope appears to be embracing forms, such as the Latin mass, that seem to have been "changed" by Vatican II.

There are eight Roman Church canonical laws relating to the sacrament of orders. Briefly they are as follows:

1. You must believe that the New Testament teaches that there is a visible and external priesthood:
    a. with the power of consecrating and offering the true body and blood of our Lord.
    b. with the power of forgiving and retaining sins.
2. You must believe that there are other orders, greater and lesser.
3. You must believe that order is a sacrament instituted by Christ.
4. You must believe that those receiving ordination also receive the Holy Spirit.
5. You must believe in the "sacred unction" used in the ordination and that once a priest, always a priest; he cannot return to being a layman.

6. You must believe that within the Roman Church there is a hierarchy divinely instituted, consisting of bishops, priests, and ministers.

7. You must believe that bishops outrank priests.

8. You must believe that bishops, "assumed by the authority of the Roman pontiff" are true and legitimate bishops.

Summary of Waterworth's book, previously cited, pp. 172-174. You must believe all of this or you are anathema (accursed, damned)!

Examination Time

Let's examine some of this stuff.

Regarding **Number 1,** what does "a visible and external priesthood" mean? I understand the "visible" part of it. They are to be seen, but what does the "external" mean? Literally it means "outside of." This, I think, is a great description of the Roman priest. He is outside of the true church of Christ. As taught and practiced by the Roman Church, this is not a Christian Church office or activity. We will look at the biblical structure of the church later.

As to having the power of consecrating and offering the true body of Christ, this is an abomination to the finished work of Christ, who, as our great High Priest, offered Himself upon the cross, once, for the payment of the sins of man (see Hebrews 9:25, 10:13, 10:26.) To appropriate His payment on our behalf for our sin, we must believe in Him, alone, as revealed in Scripture alone.

Incidentally, the magical phrase, "Hocus Pocus," comes from this ceremony of "consecration." For centuries the Latin tongue was used for the incantations used over the elements, which supposedly changed them into the Lord's body and blood. Someone merely made up some Latin sounding words (Hocus Pocus) to do their own "magical incantations."

What about "forgiving and retaining sin?" The Roman Church likes to build on Matthew 16:18; 18:16, and John 20:23, claiming this was when the apostles received the authority to forgive and retain sin. The Roman Church claims that this authority came down to them by apostolic succession. No where in Scripture is this supported.

This "authority" did not pass beyond the apostles because the Word of God, the Bible, was complete. According to Christ, the apostles, the Bible and the "Church Fathers" were to be followed for faith and practice. We will discuss this in the section devoted to Scripture verses Tradition and Church teaching.

- **Number 2** talks about "orders" (other than the priesthood) greater or lesser. From Trent came eight orders total. They are bishop, priest, deacon, sub deacon, acolyth, exorcist, tonsure and porter.

Note the exorcist's duties:

> The matter of this order is the delivery of a book of exorcisms, (to the exorcist) either a Pontifical or Missal. The form is in the words following: "Take this and commit it to memory, and have power to impose hands on persons possessed, be they baptized or catechumens." The power of the exorcists was to expel devils out of persons possessed, or to restrain them, by the imposition of their hands, and various prayers, together with holy water. This order seems now surpressed, and its powers transferred to priests; but priests cannot exorcise it without a special license from the bishop. Great abuse, such as the avarice of the exorcist (stated by Peter Dens a Roman Church theologian) and the credulity of the people, called for the extinction of the order (*Delineation of Roman Catholicism* by Rev. Charles Elliott, D.D. 1851 pp 454-455).

A book of prayers and incantations was delivered to the exorcist. More hocus pocus! The office of exorcist has been done away with because of avarice. Excuse me, isn't a form of avarice the motivation for all "magicians?" The Roman Church, itself, admits it was a phony office. The Roman Church admits "fallibility" by doing away with this office.

That said, all candidates for baptism must be exorcised first of their demonic possession or influence–even little babies.

Do you remember what Jesus said about vain, repetitious prayers?

> And in praying use not vain repetitions, as the Gentiles do: for they think that they shall be heard for their much speaking (Matthew 6:7).

When you look at the Roman Pontifical or the missal, you see preprinted prayers and scripted antics for the stage. The same prayers are chanted over and over again while the priests go through the same moves, over and over again, in the prescribed costumes. In the sacrament of extreme unction, it is not the prayers that are effective but the words and ritual pursued incantations and magical moves. The Roman rites are mere sorcery.

• **Number 3:** No where in Scripture is it said that "orders" were established by Christ.

• **Number 4:** You must believe that through the magical incantations and mumbo jumbo, those being ordained receive the Holy Spirit. This is another intensely abominable position and lie by the Roman Church. The Holy Spirit is received only by faith in Christ as Savior. When we believe we are regenerated, born again, and we receive a new heart; the Holy Spirit indwells us. Only believers and all believers have the Holy Spirit.

> And hope putteth not to shame; because the love of God hath been shed abroad in our hearts through the Holy Spirit which was given unto us (Romans 5:5 ASV).

> For the law of the Spirit of life in Christ Jesus made me free from the law of sin and of death. For what the law could not do, in that it was weak through the flesh, God, sending his own Son in the likeness of sinful flesh and for sin, condemned sin in the flesh: that the ordinance of the law might be fulfilled in us, who walk not after the flesh, but after the Spirit. For they that are after the flesh mind the things of the flesh; but they that are after the Spirit the things of the Spirit. For the mind of the flesh is death; but the mind of the Spirit is life and peace: because the mind of the flesh is enmity against God; for it is not subject to the law of God, neither indeed can it be: and they that are in the flesh cannot please God. But ye are not in the flesh but in the Spirit, if so be that the Spirit of God dwelleth in you. But if any man hath not the Spirit of Christ, he is none of his. And if Christ is in you, the body is dead because of sin; but the spirit is life because of righteousness. But if the Spirit of him that raised up Jesus from the dead dwelleth in you, he that raised up Christ Jesus from the dead shall give life also to your mortal bodies through his Spirit that dwelleth in you (Romans 8:2-11 ASV).

> But what saith it? The word is nigh thee, in thy mouth, and in thy heart: that is, the word of faith, which we preach: because if thou shalt confess with thy mouth Jesus as Lord, and shalt believe in thy heart that God raised him from the dead, thou shalt be saved: for with the heart man believeth unto righteousness; and with the mouth confession is made unto salvation. For the scripture saith, Whosoever believeth on him shall not be put to shame (Romans 10:8-11).

The Holy Spirit is given to no one through rites, ritual, incantations, or play acting. He is given: "Sola fidae" (only by faith); Sola Gratia (only by grace); Sola Scriptura (only by Scripture).

- **Number 5:** That through the sacred unction a person who becomes a priest is a priest for life, he cannot return to being a layman. Well, I guess the infallible church has committed another "fallible." I have personally worked with two ex-priests. They left the priesthood to get married, but both were still welcomed into the Roman Church as laymen.

- **Numbers 6 & 7:** Okay! I can accept these. They want them, fine, but it has nothing to do with the Church of Jesus Christ. This is a good time, though, to consider the misuse of two words by the Roman Church. These words are "episkopos," and "presbytyr." These are Greek words.

Episkopos means "overseer," it has been interpreted by the Roman Church, some Protestant Churches, some Bible versions also, as meaning "bishop." Where this word bishop comes from is beyond me. It is hard to get it out of *episkopos*.

The term *presbytyr* means "elder." The Roman Church says that the word means "priest." There is no way you can, in either Greek or other sources make this word mean priest. The Greek word for "priest" was *Ierus*.

The Roman Church has made two offices out of these words, bishop and priest. However, in the Bible there are three words that are synonymous in this regard: pastor (shepherd); overseer (bishop) and elder (presbytyr).

> For ye were going astray like sheep; but are now returned unto the Shepherd **and** [overseer] of your souls (1 Peter 2:25 ASV).

This verse refers to Jesus Christ. He is our great overseer (episkopos) and shepherd (pastor) of our souls. These responsibilities also exist in the local church. The elder/overseer/shepherd is a leader in the **local** church. Christ did not institute large international churches or denominations. He instituted the local church.

- **Number 8:** The phrase "assumed by the authority of the Roman pontiff" is interesting. The word "assumed" means to "put on" to "assume a role," it is something fictitious according to Webster's New World Dictionary. It is an act. When you see a herd of priests prancing around the front of the church going through all of their stuff, it reminds you of a Broadway musical from the Fred Astaire era. For "oldies" like me, it is reminiscent of the Radio City Rockettes.

The Real Church

The Mystery

> The Spirit of the Lord is upon me, because he anointed me to preach good tidings to the poor: He hath sent me to proclaim release to the captives, And recovering of sight to the blind, To set at liberty them that are bruised, To proclaim the acceptable year of the Lord. And he closed the book, and gave it back to the attendant, and sat down: and the eyes of all in the synagogue were fastened on him. And he began to say unto them, "Today hath this scripture been fulfilled in your ears" (Luke 4:16-21 ASV).

After His being tempted by the Devil, Christ returned to Nazareth, went into the Synogogue and read from Isaiah 61. This is a long passage that is a prophecy about the Lord coming with salvation for the nation Israel. Further, end times judgment is discussed with emphasis on Israel.

The portion that Christ quoted, however, is not limited in any way to Israel other than the "in context" cite in Isaiah 61. There is a reason for this; it is the beginning of the revelation of a mystery. Follow along and let's get to the bottom of this.

It Is Sunday About 2,000 Years Ago

I magine that you are in Jerusalem; it is Sunday and it is 2,000 years ago. There, coming down from the Mount of Olives and through the eastern gate in the wall that surrounds the city, a man rides down the street on the foal of a donkey.

> And when they drew nigh unto Jerusalem, and came unto Bethphage, unto the mount of Olives, then Jesus sent two disciples, saying unto them, Go into the village that is over against you, and straightway ye shall find an ass tied, and a colt with her: loose them, and bring them unto me. And if any one say aught unto you, ye shall say, The Lord hath need of them; and straightway he will send them. Now this is come to pass, that it might be fulfilled which was spoken through the prophet, saying, Tell ye the daughter of Zion, Behold, thy King cometh unto thee, Meek, and riding upon an ass, And upon a colt the foal of an ass. And the disciples went, and did even as Jesus appointed them, and brought the ass, and the colt, and put on them their garments; and he sat thereon. And the most part of the multitude spread their garments in the way; and others cut branches from the trees, and spread them in the way. And the multitudes that went before him, and that followed, cried, saying, Hosanna to the son of David: Blessed is he that cometh in the name of the Lord; Hosanna in the highest. And when he was come into Jerusalem, all the city was stirred, saying, Who is this? And the multitudes said, This is the prophet, Jesus, from Nazareth of Galilee (Matthew 21:1-11 ASV).

Just What Is Happening?

What is it that you are seeing? You are seeing an ancient prophesy come to life. In Isaiah 62:11 and Zechariah 9:9, this event was predicted. It is Jesus Christ, Son of God, Son of Man, descendant of King David, riding into Jerusalem on Palm Sunday to claim the throne of David and rule Israel from then on.

The crowd goes wild in anticipation. "Hosanna, hosanna," they shout. It is a real celebration, the Messiah is here. Their King has arrived! Israel will shine forth!

> And when he drew nigh, he saw the city and wept over it, saying, If thou hadst known in this day, even thou, the things which belong unto peace! but now they are hid from thine eyes. For the days shall come upon thee, when thine enemies shall cast up a bank about thee, and compass thee round, and keep thee in on every side, and shall dash thee to the ground, and thy children within thee; and they shall not leave in thee one stone upon another; because thou knewest not the time of thy visitation (Luke 19:41-44 ASV).

Whoa! Maybe not, huh! Instead of the King taking His throne and Israel shining forth, it looks as if destruction is in the future for Jerusalem. How does this fit with the ancient prophesy?

This week, which began with Jesus riding into Jerusalem as King on the back of a donkey, is the most momentous and important week in human history. The Jews rejected Him as King, He underwent three trials (the Jews, Herod, and the Romans), He was crucified, died and was buried–and the following Sunday (what we call Easter) He was raised from the dead.

What a wonderful thing, though, for the rest of us! Because of His rejection as King by Israel, the mystery starts to reveal itself. Some of Isaiah 61 can be seen to apply to the rest of us. This is for our great benefit, as without it, we would have been doomed. It is a mystery of God that is now being revealed to man.

> And as they spake these things, he himself stood in the midst of them, and saith unto them, Peace be unto you. But they were terrified and affrighted, and supposed that they beheld a spirit. And he said unto them, Why are ye troubled? and wherefore do questionings arise in your heart? See my hands and my feet, that it is I myself: handle me, and see; for a spirit hath not flesh and bones, as ye behold me having. And when he had said this, he showed them his hands and his feet. And while they still disbelieved for joy, and wondered, he said unto them, Have ye here anything to eat? And they gave him a piece of a broiled fish. And he took it, and ate before them. And he said unto them, These are my words which I spake unto you, while I was yet with you, that all things must needs be fulfilled, which are written in the law of Moses, and the prophets, and the psalms, concerning me (Luke 26:36-44 ASV).

This event takes place in Jerusalem; the disciples and others are there. The three women and Peter have already witnessed the vacant tomb, and Jesus has talked to the two disciples on the road to Emmaus.

Here He opens their minds to understand God's Word. Remember Adam? It is important that they understand; nothing has changed about the paramount importance of God's Word since the beginning. Look at what is promised: "repentance and forgiveness of sins" would be proclaimed in the name of Christ to all nations – that means all of us, not just Israel. The way of salvation is now open to all of mankind!

Where does it start? Jerusalem.

> They therefore, when they were come together, asked him, saying, Lord, dost thou at this time restore the kingdom to Israel? And he said unto them, It is not for you to know times or seasons, which the Father hath set within His own authority. But ye shall receive power, when the Holy Spirit is come upon you: and ye shall be my witnesses both in Jerusalem, and in all Judaea and Samaria, and unto the uttermost part of the earth. And when he had said these things, as they were looking, he was taken up; and a cloud received him out of their sight. And while they were looking steadfastly into heaven as he went, behold, two men stood by them in white apparel; who also said, Ye men of Galilee, why stand ye looking into heaven? This Jesus, who was received up from you into heaven shall so come in like manner as ye beheld him going into heaven (Acts 1:6-11 ASV).

In answer to their question about this being the time to restore the Kingdom to Israel, Christ responds that this is not something that is within His authority nor is it something that they have need of knowing. What they need to understand is what their duties are - and that is to witness Christ to: first, Jerusalem; second, all Judea and Samaria; third, to the end of the earth. It is an unexpected ministry to which they are called. It is not service to the King, but something else. It is the beginning of the revelation of the mystery.

Everyone on the whole face of the earth is supposed to hear about Christ. What are they to hear? They are to hear about repentance and forgiveness of sins. They are to hear that the Lord Christ lives and that He is coming again.

The Mystery

Notice also that the next time anyone sees Him on earth that He will come again in the same way that He left. He does not appear in visions, apparitions, or transubstantiation. He is **not** there in the elements of the eucharist/mass.

Chapter 2 of Acts reports on the empowerment of the disciples by the Holy Spirit. A great crowd had gathered outside the Temple in Jerusalem. The disciples were there and spoke to the crowd, with Peter having the principle message. The chapter reports how all the people were of different nationalities and tongues, yet they heard the message in their own tongue because the Holy Spirit caused the disciples to speak to them in their own language. It states that about 3,000 souls were added that day. Added? Added to what? The mystery! What is the mystery?

THE MYSTERY

> The Spirit of the Lord is upon me, because he anointed me to preach good tidings to the poor: He hath sent me to proclaim release to the captives, And recovering of sight to the blind, To set at liberty them that are bruised, To proclaim the acceptable year of the Lord (Luke 4:18-19 ASV, quoting from Isaiah 61).

Here is the "captivity" that Christ will lead captive. It is the oppressed and blind. We are not speaking in the sense of the politically oppressed or physically blind, but those who are captive to death and sin. Liberty is proclaimed to us, through the mystery.

What is the mystery? Israel stumbled! It stumbled and it has, temporarily been set aside. The Gentiles have been grafted in. Israel rejected their Messiah (King) that week He rode into Jerusalem on the foal of the donkey. Their rejection resulted in the crucifixion of Christ, which was the atonement for our sin. Therefore, the Jews' rejection of Him as their Messiah resulted in the reconciliation of the world to God (Romans 11:15).

This then is the mystery:

> That the Gentiles are fellow-heirs, and fellow-members of the body, and fellow-partakers of the promise in Christ Jesus through the gospel (Ephesians 3:6 ASV).
>
> And to make all men see what is the dispensation of the mystery which for ages hath been hid in God who created all things To the intent that now unto the principalities and the powers in the heavenly places might be made known through the church the manifold wisdom of God, according to the eternal purpose which he purposed in Christ Jesus our Lord (Ephesians 3:9-11 ASV).

The Church, comprised of all peoples and nations, is the mystery now revealed. Though, this is but the bare description. The Church is the Body of Christ. All of those who belong are members, parts, of that body (see Ephesians 5:23-25). Let's examine the structure of Christ's Church, His Body.

The Rock

> He saith unto them, But who say ye that I am? And Simon Peter answered and said, Thou art the Christ, the Son of the living God. And Jesus answered and said unto him, Blessed art thou, Simon Bar-Jonah: for flesh and blood hath not revealed it unto thee, but my Father who is in heaven. And I also say unto thee, that thou art Peter, and upon this rock I will build my church; and the gates of Hades shall not prevail against it. I will give unto thee the keys of the kingdom of heaven: and whatsoever thou shalt bind on earth shall be bound in heaven; and whatsoever thou shalt loose on earth shall be loosed in heaven (Matthew 16:15-19ASV).

This is the verse upon which the Roman Catholic Church has built the apostolic succession of the Pope at Rome. Ostensibly, Peter was the first pope as Christ is here alleged to state that He was going to build His church upon the rock that is Peter. However, when you:

- Examine, closer, the translation of these verses,
- Consider further the structure/operation of the church,

You will reject this theory of popery as not scriptural. Let us examine what the Scriptures have to say about this. What is the rock upon which Christ is building His church and how is He doing this?

As stated previously, the New Testament was translated from the Greek language. The name "Peter" is "petros," and it means a small stone or pebble. The reference to "rock" is "petra," a cliff or very large rock. There is a specific contrast here. The contrast is the difference between "petros" and "petra" linguistically. "Petros" is of the male gender in the Greek language, "petra" is feminine.

The "petra" (feminine gender) is attributed to these words, found in Matthew 16:15:

"Thou art the Christ, the Son of the living God."

This is the "Petra" or "Rock" upon which the church will be built. It is Peter's "confession" of Christ. But not just Peter's, it is the confession of Christ by all who believe. The word "confession" is (linguistically) of the feminine gender. Peter is expressing His belief in Jesus as the Messiah, and the Son of God. It is his "confession" of faith.

Some would say, though, that this is a gloss, and that Peter is still being described as the initial ruler of the church. This is disproved, though, by the use of a Greek pronoun that specifically describes the church as being built upon Jesus Christ, of Jesus Christ, and by Jesus Christ, "on this rock I will build, "mou," **of myself,** my church. "Mou" is the personal genitive pronoun translated "**of** myself." So the literal translation is "and upon this rock I will build **of me** (myself) my church.

Belief in Christ and His finished work is the necessary ingredient for union with Christ's body. I am not referring to a proclamation made at baptism or any other ritual. It is the expression of faith made when the Spirit of God causes you to be regenerated. For by grace you are saved through faith, and that not of yourselves, it is a gift of God.

Here is how the Master Builder does it. He sends the Holy Spirit to convict the sinner of sin. That person then sees him/herself in the true light, guilty before God and worthy of death. He hears the gospel that tells him Christ died for his sins and that he can have His death applied to his deserved punishment and be declared righteous before God. Upon confession of Christ as his Savior and Lord, the Holy Spirit indwells him, permanently, and he is regenerated, born again, and part of the living Body of Christ, the Church.

Well, the Church will not only be built **upon** Jesus Christ, but **of** Jesus Christ. Jesus Christ is the **Builder**, the **Corner Stone**, and a **Living Stone** (as we shall see.) The Church will be built upon Him and of Him. There is no such thing as "apostolic" succession, because nothing ceases that needs to be succeeded. Christ is the Rock, the Cornerstone, and is continually building His Church, **of Him.** The material He uses are the living stones. These are people who have confessed Christ and have been born from above. They are new creations.

What do the Church Fathers have to say about this? These comments are important because the Roman Church makes them equal to Scripture. Here are the teachings of a few:

> St. Cyril in his fourth book on the Trinity says, "I believe that by the Rock you must understand the unshaken faith of the apostles."
>
> St. Hilary, Bishop of Poitiers, in his second work on the Trinity, says, "The Rock (petra) is the blessed and only Rock of the faith confessed by the mouth of St. Peter" and in his sixth book of the Trinity, he says, "It is on this Rock of the confession of faith that the Church is built."
>
> "God," says St. Jerome in his sixth book on St. Matthew, "has founded His Church on this Rock, and it is from this Rock that the apostle Peter has been named."
>
> Ambrose, the holy Archbishop of Milan (on the second chapter of the Ephesians), St. Basil of Seleucia, and the fathers of the Council of Chalcedon, teach exactly the same thing.
>
> Of all the doctors of Christian antiquity, St. Augustine occupies one of the first places for knowledge and holiness. Listen then to what he writes in his Second Treatise on the First Epistle of St. John:
>
> What do the words mean, "I will build my Church on this Rock?" On this faith, on that which said, "Thou art the Christ, the Son of the living God." In his treatise on St. John we find this most significant phrase "On this Rock which thou hast confessed I will build my Church, since Christ was the Rock."
>
> (These quotes are from a speech given by Bishop Josip Strossmayer at Vatican 1, 1870.)

Christ is the builder of the Church and it is of Himself. Everything "keys" off of Christ, the Cornerstone. As we will see, Peter is a foundation stone along with the other 11 Disciples/Apostles. There is also one other type of stone to become acquainted with.

> So put away all malice and all deceit and hypocrisy and envy and all slander. Like newborn infants, long for the pure spiritual milk, that by it you may grow up to salvation— if indeed you have tasted that the Lord is good. As you come to him, a living stone rejected by men but in the sight of God chosen and precious, **you yourselves like living stones are being built up as a spiritual house,** to be a holy priesthood, to

offer spiritual sacrifices acceptable to God through Jesus Christ. For it stands in Scripture: Putting away therefore all wickedness, and all guile, and hypocrisies, and envies, and all evil speakings, as newborn babes, long for the spiritual milk which is without guile, that ye may grow thereby unto salvation; if ye have tasted that the Lord is gracious: unto whom coming, a living stone, rejected indeed of men, but with God elect, precious, ye also, as living stones, are built up a spiritual house, to be a holy priesthood, to offer up spiritual sacrifices, acceptable to God through Jesus Christ. Because it is contained in scripture, Behold, I lay in Zion a chief corner stone, elect, precious: And he that believeth on him shall not be put to shame. For you therefore that believe is the preciousness: but for such as disbelieve, The stone which the builders rejected, The same was made the head of the corner; and, A stone of stumbling, and a rock of offence (1 Peter 2:1-8 ASV).

Peter, by his "confession" of belief showed that he was a living stone. If you have believed in Jesus Christ as your Lord and Savior, then you have become a "living stone," a living stone that is part of a spiritual house. That house is the church. You, personally, become a temple of God in that the Spirit of God indwells you (see 1 Corinthians 3:16-17). The church where **believers** gather becomes a temple of God, in that He is there with them (Ephesians 2:19-21).

As believers, we become a **Royal Priesthood.** Both concepts apply; each believer is part of Royalty and is a Priest. Why is this so? We are living stones built upon the foundation of the apostles, which foundation is "cornered" or "keyed" by the Chief Cornerstone, Jesus Christ, our **High Priest.** The picture here is that all of these "stones" are part of each other. It is a picture of all believers joined, inseparably to Christ. Jesus is the "key" to loosing, binding, and heaven.

Jesus Christ is Prophet, Priest, King, Shepherd, Savior, Redeemer, Sustainer, and more. His Priesthood is after the order of Melchizedek, who was both Priest and King (Hebrews 7:17.) Since we are joined to Christ, we are Priests that are part of the Royal Lineage.

Believers are called a "people for his own possession." Remember, there are only two classes of Priesthood: the High King Priest, Jesus Christ – our Rock, and each living believer.

Each believer is a Royal Priest. Believers are part of, and unified with Jesus Christ "because we are members of his body" (Ephesians 5:30 ASV).

Believers have, right now, and at anytime, access to the Throne Room of God, the dwelling place of God the Father in heaven, through Christ. We may lay our petitions at His feet, personally! Christ is our intercessor, our high Priest. He provides the access. No other assistance is necessary, no other assistance is effective, no other assistance is allowed, no other assistance exists, except by imaginative fraud perpetrated by false teachers and false religions.

Let's now examine how the Church is to function.

Jesus Christ,
the One Sacrifice

Again, put yourself back at that week 2000 years ago when Jesus rode into Jerusalem upon a donkey. It is now a few days later, the triumphal entry and His three trials are past events and we see Him, beaten and bloody, dragging His cross towards Golgotha to be crucified. In His three-part-role of Prophet, King, and Priest, it is as High Priest that He is now involved.

It is not as a priest of the Levitical variety, but of the Order of Melchizedek. Further, His office of Priest is forever and it is as High Priest that He serves:"Thou art a priest for ever after the order of Melchizedek" (Hebrews 5:6 ASV).

When Jesus arrived at Golgotha with the entourage keeping pace with Him, He was nailed to His cross and it was then placed into position. He gave up His spirit later that day, and died. It is in the role of both High Priest and sacrificial victim in which He was then involved. As High Priest, He offered the sacrifice: Himself. As the victim: He died, giving His blood as atonement (covering) for the sins of man.

Keep in mind that the "standard" for acceptable sacrificial victims was that they were to be without flaw.

> Knowing that ye were redeemed, not with corruptible things, with silver or gold, from your vain manner of life handed down from your fathers; but with precious blood, as of a lamb without spot, even the blood of Christ (1 Peter 1:18-19 ASV).

Woops! As a side note, re-read this verse. Think about it the next time you think you should give money to buy your way out of sin or to help a relative out of that fairy-tale-land of Purgatory. You cannot be redeemed by silver or gold or works, only the precious blood of Christ.

Jesus Christ is both fully man and fully God. As man, He is of the race of the second Adam and was indwelt and sanctified (set apart—referring to His humanity) by the Holy Spirit prior to birth. He was sanctified from committing sin by the power of

God through the Holy Spirit. He was tempted as are we, but without sin. Without sin refers to any and all thought, word, or deed.

His virgin birth also sanctified or set Him apart from original sin. He was never part of the race of the first Adam. All of this needs to be thoroughly understood, so that what follows will make since.

> By which will we have been sanctified through the offering of the body of Jesus Christ once for all. And every priest indeed standeth day by day ministering and offering often times the same sacrifices, the which can never take away sins: but he, when he had offered one sacrifice for sins forever, sat down on the right hand of God; henceforth expecting till his enemies be made the footstool of his feet. For by one offering he hath perfected forever them that are sanctified And the Holy Spirit also beareth witness to us; for after he hath said, This is the covenant that I will make with them After those days, saith the Lord: I will put my laws on their heart, And upon their mind also will I write them; then saith he, And their sins and their iniquities will I remember no more. Now where remission of these is, there is no more offering for sin (Hebrews 10:10-18 ASV).

This sacrifice is sufficient for all sin(s), past, present, and future for all men, but applies only to those who believe. We are discussing how the sacrifice applies to the church, which is no different than any other application, except it will show us how Christ manages His body, the Church.

Remember the problem Adam got us into when he rebelled against God by disobeying (not believing) God's Word? Then remember the trouble that Moses got himself into by not believing God's Word and striking the rock rather than speaking to it as instructed? God expects us to believe His Word.

Why do I bring this up now? Because the sacrifice of Christ was sufficient for all sin. God says, in His Word, that Christ offered one sacrifice for sins for all time, and sat down at the right hand of God. **One sacrifice** for sins for **all** time! In the eucharist/mass, the Roman Catholic Church thinks that they are killing Christ over and over again as a sacrifice. God says that Christ's one sacrifice was sufficient. The Roman Catholic Church says (through their rituals of the eucharist and mass) that God is a liar.

Pay attention to the one you believe will win this argument and get over on His side. You do not want to be a loser. Notice this portion of the passage again:

> [Christ] SAT DOWN AT THE RIGHT HAND OF GOD, waiting from that time onward UNTIL HIS ENEMIES BE MADE A FOOTSTOOL FOR HIS FEET (HEBREWS 10:12, 13).

At the day of the "footstool" you will see many Deacons, Priests, Prelates, Cardinals, and Popes weeping and gnashing their teeth wishing that they had believed the Word. One sacrifice is all that our High Priest needed to make. One sacrifice, and it was of Himself. To say that this sacrifice must go on is a direct attack upon the person, being, and character of God, Almighty, His only begotten Son, the Lord Jesus Christ, and the Holy Spirit. One should shudder at any idea of being so involved.

Remember in the "Rock" confession that we all (including Christ) are "Living Stones" fitted together with Him in His body, called the Church? Keep in mind that He, our High Priest, is seated right now, at the right hand of God the Father. Christ has, right now, charge of all things concerning the Church. Here is how He exercises that authority.

> THIS IS THE COVENANT THAT I WILL MAKE WITH THEM AFTER THOSE DAYS, SAYS THE LORD: I WILL PUT MY LAWS UPON THEIR HEART, AND ON THEIR MIND I WILL WRITE THEM (Hebrews 10:16).

If you are a "believer," you are a member of the Body of Christ, the Church. If you are a member of that Body, you are a Living Stone. If you are a Living Stone, then you have the Laws of God on your heart and written upon your mind. If you are these things, then you are also of the Royal Priesthood with constant access to the throne room of God, where you can directly lay your prayers. You are one of the poor captives that Christ has set free!

Christ is right now and constantly in charge of His Church. He is changing and guiding our service in it and to it by His Law, which is upon our hearts and written on our minds. He is doing this through the Holy Spirit that indwells us. He indwells you, that is, if you have come to the point of believing upon Christ as your Lord and Savior.

We have a two-class priesthood: our High Priest, Jesus Christ, constantly seated at the right hand of God Almighty; and the believer priest, the Living Stones of the visible Church. That is all; there are no more priests than this. They are all **internal** to the Church, not external as the Roman Church catechism admits of their priests. They are external to the Church, not part of it!

The Universal Church Versus the Local Church

So far we have been talking about the "universal" church. The universal Church is the whole body of believers in the world plus those present with the Lord in heaven. Those that have left their bodies to be present with the Lord in Heaven since the beginning of the "Church" age are still functioning members of the universal church. They, and all believers, will be judges of the world and angels.

> Or know ye not that the saints shall judge the world? And if the world is judged by you, are ye unworthy to judge the smallest matters? Know ye not that we shall judge angels? How much more, things that pertain to this life? (1 Corinthians 6:2-3 ASV).

This will occur when Christ returns to earth to set up His 1000-year-reign as King. This period of time is called the Millennium.

There is the "visible" church also. It is the visible or "local" church that functions to build up the Body. We need to examine it. All believers should be involved in ministry to and through it. Not all who attend a local church are believers, nor is it, in a way, desirable that they all be. Reaching unbelievers for Christ is a ministry that the Church is called to perform. One way to reach the unbeliever is to have him/her sit under a Bible teaching ministry, to hear the Word of God. I, personally, was affected by such a ministry.

> The Spirit of the Lord is upon me, Because he anointed me to preach good tidings to the poor: He hath sent me to proclaim release to the captives, And recovering of sight to the blind, To set at liberty them that are bruised, To proclaim the acceptable year of the Lord (Luke 4:18, 19).

The captives, blind and the oppressed are to be sought out by activities of the Church empowered by the Holy Spirit. These activities began in Jerusalem and will spread to the ends of the earth before Jesus returns in His Kingdom.

Here is day one of the visible church. That's right, the very first day of the visible or local church. Imagine that you are standing outside the Temple in Jerusalem. It is fifty-eight days since you watched Jesus ride into Jerusalem on that donkey. It is fifty days since His resurrection.

> Now there were dwelling at Jerusalem Jews, devout men, from every nation under heaven. And when this sound was heard, the multitude came together, and were confounded, because that every man heard them speaking in his own language. And they were all amazed and marvelled, saying, Behold, are not all these that speak Galilaeans? And how hear we, every man in our own language wherein we were born? Parthians and Medes and Elamites, and the dwellers in Mesopotamia, in Judaea and Cappadocia, in Pontus and Asia, in Phrygia and Pamphylia, in Egypt and the parts of Libya about Cyrene, and sojourners from Rome, both Jews and proselytes, Cretans and Arabians, we hear them speaking in our tongues the mighty works of God (Acts 2:1-12 ASV).

Notice where all these people are from. The places specifically mentioned stretch from modern Iran to Italy. Many of these people placed their faith in Jesus Christ as their Savior and Lord that day, 3000 it says in verse 41. When they returned to their home cities, they took the message of Christ with them and proclaimed it in their local Synagogues. Later missionaries from the Jerusalem church came, preached the same message and helped them establish local churches.

Where did these missionaries come from? Who were they?

Jesus had instructed His disciples to remain in Jerusalem until empowered by the Holy Spirit. They did so, meeting in an "upper room." There were 120 of them.

> Then returned they unto Jerusalem from the mount called Olivet, which is nigh unto Jerusalem, a Sabbath day's journey off. And when they were come in, they went up into the upper chamber, where they were abiding; both Peter and John and James and Andrew, Philip and Thomas, Bartholomew and Matthew, James the son of Alphaeus, and Simon the Zealot, and Judas the son of James. These all with one accord continued steadfastly in prayer, with the women, and Mary the mother of Jesus, and with his brethren. And in these days Peter stood up in the midst of the brethren, and said (and there was a multitude of persons gathered together, about a hundred and twenty) (Acts 1:12-15 ASV).

The initial missionaries came out of this group. Later the Apostle Paul was added, as well as others, and the church planting spread throughout the world. It spread as Christ instructed them. Beginning at Jerusalem, Judea, Samaria, and to the ends of the earth. The effort began **after** the Church had been empowered by the Holy Spirit. The Holy Spirit was and is working at the direction of the Head of the Church, Jesus Christ, who is seated at the right hand of God.

Each local (visible) Church was set up as an independent Church, created for ministry of the Word of God to that particular community. To see this clearly, you must understand the meaning of the word **Elder,** which has been perverted into the word "priest" by the Roman Church. It is the Greek word "presbyter."

Elder, of course, was used in the Bible to designate "older" people. However, it was also used to designate a "civil" office, such as ambassador, or a representative/leader of a group of people. In captivity, Israel had "elders" that God directed Moses to communicate with, when God was ready to bring Israel out of Egypt to the Promised Land (see Exodus 3:16). They had the duties of "shepherd (pastor), and overseer (episkopos or bishop.) That said, whenever you see the term shepherd or bishop in the Bible, it is referring to an Elder.

Later, God told Moses to choose out 70 elders to help him (Moses) lead and rule the people in the wilderness.

> And Jehovah said unto Moses, Gather unto me seventy men of the elders of Israel, whom thou knowest to be the elders of the people, and officers over them; and bring them unto the tent of meeting, that they may stand there with thee (Numbers 11:16 ASV).

These seventy men comprised the Sanhedrin. It was the seventy elders, Sanhedrin, that exercised civil government during Christ's ministry on earth. They were subject both to Herod and to Rome, but they were pretty much allowed a free hand as long as peace and order were maintained.

We need to examine, though, the meaning of Ambassador and its relevance to the Church. As stated above, one of the functions of an Elder could be as Ambassador.

> Wherefore if any man is in Christ, he is a new creature: the old things are passed away; behold, they are become new. But all things are of

> God, who reconciled us to himself through Christ, and gave unto us the ministry of reconciliation; to wit, that God was in Christ reconciling the world unto Himself, not reckoning unto them their trespasses, and having committed unto us the word of reconciliation. We are ambassadors therefore on behalf of Christ, as though God were entreating by us: we beseech you on behalf of Christ, be ye reconciled to God. Him who knew no sin he made to be sin on our behalf; that we might become the righteousness of God in him (2 Corinthians 5:17-20 ASV).

An Ambassador existed for **one purpose only**, and that was to do the will of his Lord. He would have known his Lord very well, so he could make decisions in accord with his will. As you see, **all who are born from above** (New Creations) are Ambassadors for Christ with the ministry of the message of reconciliation. That is the purpose of salvation. It is to carry the message from the Word of God to the captives, the blind and the oppressed. All those enslaved to sin and death.

The message of reconciliation is preached to real people by members of the body of Christ, the local church. For this to happen, a local church must be established. You see this happening throughout the Book of Acts.

Christ instructed them in the Great Commission to make, then baptize disciples of all nations. (A disciple, by definition is a believer/learner. Note that they have to be a disciple prior to baptism.)

> Go ye therefore, and make disciples of all the nations, baptizing them into the name of the Father and of the Son and of the Holy Spirit: teaching them to observe all things whatsoever I commanded you: and lo, I am with you always, even unto the end of the world (Matthew 28:19 ASV).

It was pointed out that this was to begin in Jerusalem, then go to Judea and Samaria, then throughout the world. As you read through the Book of Acts you can see how this happened.

Through out the Gospels and to the eleventh chapter of Acts, the term Elder is used in connection with the rulers of Israel. In chapter eleven, Elder is used the first time in connection with the church.

Because of the conversions at Jerusalem on Pentecost, and the persecution of the Christians after the stoning of Stephen, men from all over the "world" went back to their homelands with the message of Christ. One of those places was Antioch. A church was founded there (Acts 11:19). It was at Antioch that the disciples were first called Christians (Acts 11:25).

The Church at Antioch learned of a terrible famine that was afflicting the Church at Jerusalem, and the disciples, each according to his ability, sent a contribution for the relief of the brothers at Jerusalem to the Elders of the Jerusalem Church. From this, and what is reported as happened elsewhere, we can infer that all the churches established in Judea and Samaria likewise had Elders. Let's look at "elsewhere."

> But as the disciples stood round about him, he rose up, and entered into the city: and on the morrow he went forth with Barnabas to Derbe. And when they had preached the gospel to that city, and had made many disciples, they returned to Lystra, and to Iconium, and to Antioch, confirming the souls of the disciples, exhorting them to continue in the faith, and that through many tribulations we must enter into the kingdom of God. And when they had appointed for them elders in every church, and had prayed with fasting, they commended them to the Lord, on whom they had believed (Acts 14:20-23 ASV).

Acts 15 records a council of the Apostles and Elders at Jerusalem over the issue of whether or not it was proper to preach the Word to Gentiles in addition to Jews. This council examined Scripture and saw that it was God's plan to do so. In this section you see the leadership position of the office of Elder in the Church.

Elders, from the aspect of ambassador/leader/teachers/overseers were appointed by the missionaries from Jerusalem. Each Church grew around them. The governance of each Church is, actively, from Christ, through the Holy Spirit, to the Elders, of that Church who are guided by the Word of God, the Bible.

> Elder (presbuteros) and bishop (episcopos = "overseer") designate the same office (cf Titus 1:7; Acts 20:17; 20:28 the former referring to the man, the latter to a function of the office). The eldership in the apostolic local churches was always plural. There is no instance of one elder in a local church. The functions of the elders are: to rule

(1 Timothy 3:4,5; 5:17); to guard the body of revealed truth from perversion and error (Titus 1:9); to "oversee" the church as a shepherd his flock (Acts 20:28; John 21:16; Hebrews 13:17; 1 Peter 5:2) (From note to Titus 1:5, The New Schofield Reference Bible on line at http://bible.crosswalk.com/Commentaries/ScofieldReferenceNotes).

DEACON

Not much is said about the office of Deacon. The qualifications for Deacon are defined in 1 Timothy 3:8-13. The term is defined by these passages: Matthew 4:11; Mark 1:13; Matthew 20:26; Romans 16:1; Ephesians 6:21; 1Thessalonians 3:2. A Deacon is one who ministers to some need. The Deacon acts as a servant. An example of this occurs early in the history of the Church.

> Now in these days, when the number of the disciples was multiplying, there arose a murmuring of the Grecian Jews against the Hebrews, because their widows were neglected in the daily ministration. And the twelve called the multitude of the disciples unto them, and said, It is not fit that we should forsake the word of God, and serve tables. Look ye out therefore, brethren, from among you seven men of good report, full of the Spirit and of wisdom, whom we may appoint over this business. But we will continue steadfastly in prayer, and in the ministry of the word. And the saying pleased the whole multitude: and they chose Stephen, a man full of faith and of the Holy Spirit, and Philip, and Prochorus, and Nicanor, and Timon, and Parmenas, and Nicolaus a proselyte of Antioch; whom they set before the apostles: and when they had prayed, they laid their hands upon them (Acts 6:1-6 ASV).

The office of Deacon is for the Church. It is also a group of men, not just a single office. They exist to take care of the material needs for the local body of Christ.

All believers, though, have the ministry of Elder/Ambassador to their local community for their local church. All believers need to be reaching out in the name of Christ to their community with the Word of Christ. I am **not** saying that all believers are Elders, but they have a duty that is attributable to the office of Elder. Further, all believers are gifted by the Holy Spirit with a ministry to serve within their local body. This is the purpose of their salvation–to serve in the local body in the manner for which they are gifted.

> But unto each one of us was the grace given according to the measure of the gift of Christ. Wherefore he saith, When he ascended on high, he led captivity captive, And gave gifts unto men (Ephesians 4:7-8 ASV).

Does this verse remind you of the one from Luke 4? It should because it is "more of the same." This is actually a quote from Psalms 68:18. Verse 19 of this Psalm explains that the Lord gave the gifts so that He could dwell among men. As we have seen, the Church is Christ's body and all believers are Living Stones in that body. All believers are unified with Christ and must be gifted by Christ so that this unity is holy and workable. The "gifts" are God-given abilities to serve a particular function, or service within the local church.

How do you become a Living Stone in the Church? You need to come to the point where you agree with the following and then place your faith in Jesus Christ as your personal Savior and Lord.

- There is none righteous, no, not one (Romans 3:10).
- For all have sinned and come short of the glory of God (Romans 3:23).
- For as by one man, sin entered the world, and death by sin, and so death passed to all men for all sinned (Romans 5:12).
- The wages of sin is death (Romans 6:23).
- But thanks be to God, that, whereas ye were servants of sin, ye became obedient from the heart to that form of teaching whereunto ye were delivered; and being made free from sin, ye became servants of righteousness. I speak after the manner of men because of the infirmity of your flesh: for as ye presented your members as servants to uncleanness and to iniquity unto iniquity, even so now present your members as servants to righteousness unto sanctification. For when ye were servants of sin, ye were free in regard of righteousness. What fruit then had ye at that time in the things whereof ye are now ashamed? For the end of those things is death (Romans 6:17-21 ASV).

- But what saith it? The word is nigh thee, in thy mouth, and in thy heart: that is, the word of faith, which we preach: because if thou shalt confess with thy mouth Jesus as Lord, and shalt believe in thy heart that God raised him from the dead, thou shalt be saved (Romans 10:8-9 ASV).

Notice the word "confess." Do you remember that is what Peter did? He confessed Christ and Christ told Him and the other disciples that His church would be built upon that confession. Every member of the Church since that point only became a member by such a confession. That is how the Church has been built, by Christ, of Christ, **not** Peter.

Have you confessed Christ as your Savior and Lord? If you have not personally settled this issue, you should talk to God right now and tell Him that you want Christ as your Lord and Savior. Tell Him that you want the forgiveness for your sins that He provides. Tell God that you want to be born of the Spirit. Your confession will make you a vital member in the body of Christ. You will be unified with Him as a Living Stone in His Body, the Church. You will be regenerated to serve Him and to tell your friends the good news of salvation, assured through the single sacrifice of Jesus Christ, our High Priest.

Tradition, Scripture, and The "Authority" of The Roman Church

Scripture and Tradition

Decree Concerning the Canonical Scriptures:

> The sacred and holy, oecumenical, and general Synod of Trent—lawfully assembled in the Holy Ghost, the same three legates of the Apostolic See presiding therein—keeping this always in view, that errors being removed, the purity itself of the Gospel be preserved in the Church; which (Gospel), before promised through the prophets in the holy Scriptures, our Lord Jesus Christ, the Son of God, first prophesied with His own mouth, and then commanded to be preached by His Apostles to every creature, [?] as the fountain of all, both saving truth, and moral Discipline; and seeing clearly that this truth and discipline are contained in the written books, and the unwritten traditions, which, received by the Apostles themselves, the Holy Ghost dictating, have come down even to us, transmitted as it were from hand to hand; (the synod) following the examples of the orthodox Fathers, receives and venerates with an equal affection of piety, and reverence, all the books both of the Old and of the New Testament—seeing that one God is the Author of both—as also the said traditions, as well those appertaining to faith as to morals, as having been dictated, either by Christ's own word of mouth, or the Holy Spirit and preserved in the Catholic Church by continuous succession (*The Sacred & Oecumenical Council of Trent,* Rev. J. Waterworth, pp. 17, 18).

> Let no one ... wresting the sacred Scripture to his own senses, presume to interpret the said sacred Scripture contrary to that sense which the holy mother Church—whose it is to judge of the true sense and interpretation of the holy Scriptures—hath held and doth hold or even contrary to the unanimous consent of the Fathers; eve though such interpretations were never [intended] to be at any time published (ibid, p. 19).

> The Gospel was to be the source of all saving truth and moral discipline. This was faithfully done: it was done by the apostles who handed on, by the spoken word of their preaching, by the example they gave, by the institutions they established, what they themselves had received—whether from the lips of Christ, from his way of life and his works, or whether they had learned it at the prompting of the Holy Spirit, it was done by those apostles and other men associated with the apostles who, under the inspiration of the same Holy Spirit, committed the message of salvation to writing.... the apostles left bishops

as their successors. They gave them "their own position of teaching authority. This Sacred Tradition, then and the Sacred Scripture of both Testaments, are like a mirror, in which the Church, during its pilgrim journey here on earth, contemplates God (*Vatican Council II*, Austen Flannery, O.P.)

Catholicism is a tradition that places great emphasis on tradition. It recognizes that the Bible itself is **a product of tradition (or, more precisely, of many traditions.)** Before there were written texts the faith was handed on through proclamation, catechesis, worship, and personal example. For Catholicism, God speaks through means such as these, not only through words but through deeds as well. History in general and the history of the Church in particular are carriers of this divine revelation. Catholicism, therefore, not only reads its Sacred Scripture, but also its own corporate life and experience. As Pope John XXIII (d 1963) once said, **"history, itself is a teacher"** (*Catholicism*, Richard P. McBride; Harper San Francisco 1994, p. 14).

Bishop Hay, a Roman Catholic, gave this explanation to the question:

"What is Tradition?" His answer was this: "The handing down from one generation to another, whether by word of mouth, or by writings, those truths revealed by Jesus Christ to his apostles, which either are not at all contained in the Holy Scriptures, or at least are not clearly contained in them."

Another Roman writer, Dr. Milner, asserted that:

The Roman Catholic rule of faith is **Scripture and Tradition,** and these are propounded and explained by the Roman Catholic Church.

(*Delineation of Roman Catholicism,* by Rev. Charles Elliott D.D., p. 96)

Here we see the Roman Church's dedication to the pre-eminence of Tradition over Scripture. As a matter of fact, since Scripture and Tradition is obviously that which is "propounded and explained by the Roman Church, the church is the pre-eminent authority on both. Both Scripture and Tradition are whatever the Roman Church wants them to be. That is the **only** interpretation you can give to the statement by the infallible Pope John XXIII. Tradition of its own corporate life and experience is equal to, nay, superior to Scripture? Is this not adding to the Word of God?

Clearly these cites about Tradition show that the Roman Church adds to the Word of God. With their rule of faith making the church the propounder and explainer of both, they continually add to the Word of God. Rather, though, I think they hold the Word of God as being an abomination. That is, they despise it.

Let's Give This Stuff A "Sherlocking"

L**et's investigate this** as would Sherlock Holmes.
- The first point, that the Gospel was to be preached to every creature, is pure silliness. Adam sinned and brought death into the world. It was not the elephants, doves, pigs or puppy dogs that needed to hear the gospel, but man. Jesus instructed His disciples and the rest of us to preach the Good News of His saving work to men, not all creatures. Am I making too big a deal of this? Seems like that was part of what "St." Francis did, was preach to the creatures. Then, what about those special days when pets and other animals are blessed by the church? It is plain goofy!
- The three passages previously quoted establish that Tradition is equal to Scripture in the Roman Church. The canon law established by the Council of Trent states that only the Church has the right to interpret the meaning. The quote from Charles Elliott's book shows that the Roman Church considers herself superior to both.
- The Canon Law from Trent references the "orthodox Fathers." This refers to the "church Fathers" from the first through fifth centuries.

Well, what about it?

Here are some words spoken by Christ concerning His Word and Tradition.

> It is written, Man shall not live by bread alone, but by every word that proceedeth out of the mouth of God (Matthew 4:4 ASV).

> And ye have made void the word of God because of your tradition (Matthew 15:6 ASV).

> The sower soweth the word. And these are they by the way side, where the word is sown; and when they have heard, straightway cometh Satan, and taketh away the word which hath been sown in them (Mark 4:14 ASV).

Make void the word of God by your tradition, which ye have delivered: and many such like things ye do (Mark 7:13 ASV).

Yea rather, blessed are they that hear the word of God, and keep it (Luke 11:28 ASV).

Verily, verily, I say unto you, He that heareth my word, and believeth him that sent me, hath eternal life, and cometh not into judgment, but hath passed out of death into life (John 5:24 ASV).

And ye have not his word abiding in you: for whom he sent him ye believe not. Ye search the scriptures, because ye think that in them ye have eternal life; and these are they which bear witness of me; and ye will not come to me, that ye may have life (John 5:38-40 ASV).

If ye abide in my word, then are ye truly my disciples; and ye shall know the truth, and the truth shall make you free (John 8:31-32 ASV).

Verily, verily, I say unto you, If a man keep my word, he shall never see death (John 8:51 ASV).

He that rejecteth me, and receiveth not my sayings, hath one that judgeth him: the word that I spake, the same shall judge him in the last day (John 12:45 ASV).

If a man love me, he will keep my word: and my Father will love him, and we will come unto him, and make our abode with him. He that loveth me not keepeth not my words: and the word which ye hear is not mine, but the Father's who sent me (John 14:23-24 ASV).

Already ye are clean because of the word which I have spoken unto you. Abide in me, and I in you (John 15:3-4 ASV).

Remember the word that I said unto you, A servant is not greater than his lord. If they persecuted me, they will also persecute you; if they kept my word, they will keep yours also (John 15:20 ASV).

I manifested thy name unto the men whom thou gavest me out of the world: thine they were, and thou gavest them to me; and they have kept thy word. Now they know that all things whatsoever thou hast given me are from thee: for the words which thou gavest me I have given unto them (John 17:6-8 ASV).

I have given them thy word; and the world hated them, because they are not of the world, even as I am not of the world (John 17:14 ASV).

Sanctify them in the truth: thy word is truth. As thou didst send me into the world, even so sent I them into the world. And for their sakes I sanctify myself, that they themselves also may be sanctified in truth. Neither for these only do I pray, but for them also that believe on me through their word (John 17:17-20 ASV).

It seems to me that Christ could not be clearer. Traditions of men only lead man to destruction. If you love the Lord you will keep His Word. In order to keep His Word you must know it. In order to know it you must read it. The Bible is His Word. It is the single source of information that can lead you to salvation.

Tradition

There are only two references to Tradition in the rest of the New Testament:

> Take heed lest there shall be any one that maketh spoil of you through his philosophy and vain deceit, after the tradition of men, after the rudiments of the world, and not after Christ: for in him dwelleth all the fullness of the Godhead bodily (I Corinthians 2:8-9 ASV).

> Now we command you, brethren, in the name of our Lord Jesus Christ, that ye withdraw yourselves from every brother that walketh disorderly, and not after the tradition which they received of us. For yourselves know how ye ought to imitate us: for we behaved not ourselves disorderly among you; neither did we eat bread for nought at any man's hand, but in labor and travail, working night and day, that we might not burden any of you: not because we have not the right, but to make ourselves an ensample unto you, that ye should imitate us. For even when we were with you, this we commanded you, If any will not work, neither let him eat. For we hear of some that walk among you disorderly, that work not at all, but are busybodies. Now them that are such we command and exhort in the Lord Jesus Christ, that with quietness they work, and eat their own bread. But ye, brethren, be not weary in well-doing. And if any man *obeyeth not our word by this epistle,* note that man, that ye have no company with him, to the end that he may be ashamed. And yet count him not as an enemy, but admonish him as a brother (2 Thessalonians 3:6-15 ASV).

The following is summarized from Dr. Elliott's book, *Delineation of Roman Catholiscism,* p. 97.

- The word "tradition" comes from the Latin word "traditio," which means word of mouth without written memorials, or it means anything offered orally from age to age.
- The Greek word (the language in which the New Testament was originally written) is Paradosis. This word means precept, instruction, ordinance, delivered either orally or in writing. The compound root of this word is "paradidomi," to deliver from one to another, to deliver down, and is from "para" down, and "didomi" to give, extend, deliver from one to another.

The Apostle Paul wrote 2 Thessalonians under the inspiration of the Holy Spirit. These instructions are from God through Paul.

They are **only** "paradosis," **delivered** by Paul. These "traditions" are "paradosis" or instructions from God, Himself.

> "Paradosis," tradition, is the same with "dogma," a doctrine; and "paradidonai," to deliver down, is the same with "didaskein, to teach, say the grammarians. The "paradotheisa pistis," the **faith delivered** is the same with the traditions which you were taught, mentioned by the Apostle Paul (*History of Romanism*, John Dowling).

> Beloved, while I was giving all diligence to write unto you of our common salvation, I was constrained to write unto you exhorting you to contend earnestly for the faith which **was once for all delivered** unto the saints. For there are certain men crept in privately, even they who were of old written of beforehand unto this condemnation, ungodly men, turning the grace of our God into lasciviousness, and denying our only Master and Lord, Jesus Christ (Jude 3-4 ASV).

Now here is a very interesting passage as it relates to not only Scripture verses Tradition, but it identifies those who place Tradition in the Latin sense and the pre-eminence of the church's propounding and teaching on equal terms with Scripture as false teachers, ungodly men. How so?

The word "delivered" is paradosis, or tradition. Notice it says that our faith was **once and for all** delivered. Once and for all, it is recorded in Scripture.

Look at Christ's words. The following is just a sample:

> If a man love me, he will keep my word: and my Father will love him, and we will come unto him, and make our abode with him. He that loveth me not keepeth not my words: and the word which ye hear is not mine, but the Father's who sent me (John 14:23-24 ASV).

These are not oral traditions. The writers of the New Testament were inspired, guided, enlightened by the Holy Spirit in recalling these things.

> Howbeit when he, the Spirit of truth, is come, he shall guide you into all the truth (John 16:13 ASV).

Here are some references to the Word or Scriptures, in the balance of the New Testament.

> Brethren, it was needful that the Scripture should be fulfilled, which the Holy Spirit spake before by the mouth of David concerning Judas, who was guide to them that took Jesus. For he was numbered among us, and received his portion in this ministry (Acts 1:16-17 ASV).

Escape From Paganism

> Now the passage of the Scripture which he was reading was this, He was led as a sheep to the slaughter; And as a lamb before his shearer is dumb, So he openeth not his mouth: In his humiliation his judgment was taken away: His generation who shall declare? For his life is taken from the earth. And the eunuch answered Philip, and said, I pray thee, of whom speaketh the prophet this? Of himself, or of some other? And Philip opened his mouth, and beginning from this Scripture, preached unto him Jesus. (Acts 8:32-35 ASV).

> For what saith the scripture? And Abraham believed God, and it was reckoned unto him for righteousness (Romans 4:3 ASV).

> For the scripture saith unto Pharaoh, For this very purpose did I raise thee up, that I might show in thee my power, and that my name might be published abroad in all the earth. So then he hath mercy on whom he will, and whom he will be hardeneth (Romans 9:17-18 ASV).

> For the scripture saith, Whosoever believeth on him shall not be put to shame. For there is no distinction between Jew and Greek: for the same Lord is Lord of all, and is rich unto all that call upon him: for, Whosoever shall call upon the name of the Lord shall be saved (Romans 10:11-13 ASV).

> And the scripture, foreseeing that God would justify the Gentiles by faith, preached the gospel beforehand unto Abraham, saying, In thee shall all the nations be blessed. So then they that are of faith are blessed with the faithful Abraham (Galatians 3:8-9 ASV).

Does it not amaze you that the passages above refer to the Old Testament? The words in the Old Testament were "paradosis" (tradition) delivered to their hearers by God, but later recorded in writing under the inspiration of the Holy Spirit, once and for all!

> Every scripture inspired of God is also profitable for teaching, for reproof, for correction, for instruction which is in righteousness. That the man of God may be complete, furnished completely unto every good work (2 Timothy 3:16-17 ASV).

> Or think ye that the scripture speaketh in vain? Doth the spirit which he made to dwell in us long unto envying? But he giveth more grace. Wherefore the scripture saith, God resisteth the proud, but giveth grace to the humble. Be subject therefore unto God; but resist the devil, and he will flee from you (James 4:5-7 ASV).

> Because it is contained in scripture, Behold, I lay in Zion a chief corner stone, elect, precious: And he that believeth on him shall not be put to shame. For you therefore that believe is the preciousness: but for such

as disbelieve, the stone which the builders rejected, The same was made the head of the corner; and, A stone of stumbling, and a rock of offence (1 Peter 2:6-8 ASV).

Knowing this first, that no prophecy of scripture is of private interpretation. For no prophecy ever came by the will of man: but men spake from God, being moved by the Holy Spirit (2 Peter 1:20-21 ASV).

Did The Orthodox Fathers Sanction Tradition Over Scripture?

The **Roman Church claims** that the Orthodox Fathers of the Church were unanimous in supporting Tradition. Were they? At the Council of Trent they attempted to destroy and prohibit any writings or teachings that would conflict with the "truth" propounded and taught by the church. They established the **Index Expurgatorius**. This was a list of books and passages that the Roman Church faithful were prohibited from reading. The Index was established in 1562 at the Council of Trent and retired in 1966.

Well, just what did the "orthodox Fathers" have to say about Scripture verses Tradition? Were they, in fact, unanimously agreed that the validity of Tradition equaled that of Scripture? Again I turn to the chapter on *Tradition* in Dr. Elliott's book (previously cited). This material starts on page 113 of that book. Dr. Elliot introduces this material this way:

> The writers of the first six centuries are commonly embraced in the list of the fathers. Those who were contemporary with the apostles are called apostolical fathers. These are Barnabas, Clement of Rome, Hermas, Ignatius, and Polycarp. They were all natives of the East, except Clement, and wrote in Greek.
>
> The principal Greek writers who succeeded the apostolical fathers were Justin Martyr and Irenaeus.

Here are some quotes from some of these men:

> **1.** Ignatius some say that he was about seven years old when Christ preached. He was called Theosophorus and was made Bishop of Antioch in 70 AD. He was martyred in 107 AD. He exhorted his followers to "Hold firmly to the tradition delivered by the Apostles, which had already been committed to writing, which was necessary for their preservation." In other words, the "paradosis" tradition, was now set down on paper and was now Scripture.
>
> **2.** Irenaeus, a Greek born about the year 140 AD, was a disciple of Polycarp and Papias, went to Gaul (modern France), was ordained priest, and afterwards Bishop of Lyons in the year 178. He suffered martyrdom in the year 202 or 203. He said "If it had so happened that

the apostles had left us no Scriptures, must we not then have followed the order of Tradition, which they committed to the church? (This quote is frequently used by the Roman Church to buoy up their claim to the legitimacy of Tradition and church pre-eminence.)

- But notice that Irenaeus states that "had they left us no Scriptures, then we would have had to revert to Tradition."

- But we were left with the Scriptures and therefore are not compelled or allowed to revert to unwritten Tradition.

- In another place Irenaeus declares, "We have known the method of our salvation by no others than those by whom the gospel came to us: which gospel they then truly preached; but afterward, by the will of God, they delivered to us in the Scriptures, to be for the future the foundation and pillar of our faith.'"

- More from Irenaeus: "Knowing very well that the Scriptures are perfect, for they are spoken by the word of God and His Spirit" and "Read more diligently that gospel which is given to us by the apostles; and read more diligently the prophets, and you will find every section and the whole doctrine of our Lord preached in them."

Remember, the Roman Church has declared the orthodox Fathers to be united on the issue of Tradition equaling that of Scripture. Further, they like to quote Irenaeus in support of that doctrine. We see here that they have lied. But what is new and different about this?

3. Tertullian, originally of Africa, was a Carthaginian, prebyter of Carthage, and a Latin writer. He flourished under the emperors Severus and Caracalla, from the year 194 until toward the year 216. He died about AD 220.

In a disputation with Gnostic heretics, he made the following statement: "Whether all things were made of any subject matter, I have as yet to read nowhere. Let the scroll of Hermogenes show that it is written; if it is not written, let them fear the curse allotted to such as add or diminish." He is, of course, referring to the curse of God for adding or subtracting from His word (see Deuteronomy 4:2 and Revelation 22:18).

4. Clemens of Alexandria flourished from 196 to 220 AD and died in 220. He defined ecclesiastical Tradition as "he ... obeys the Scriptures, and has entrusted his life to Truth." He further stated how the Scriptures are a perfect demonstration of faith: "Perfectly demonstrating out of the Scriptures themselves, we speak or persuade demonstratively of the faith."

5. Origen was Alexandrian and born about the year 185. He flourished until the year 252, at which time he died. In his fifth sermon on Leviticus, Origen spoke these words regarding the two Testaments: "In which every word that pertains to God may be required and discussed; and all knowledge of things be understood out of them." He stated elsewhere: "We know Jesus Christ is God, and we seek to expound the words which are spoken according to the dignity of the Person. Wherefore it is necessary for us to call the Scriptures into testimony, for our meanings and narrations without these witnesses, have no belief."

To these words Cardinal Bellarmine, writing at the end of the 16th Century stated: 'Origen speaks of the hardest questions, on which, for the most part Traditions do not treat." Bellarmine was a Roman Church apologist writing just a few years after the Council of Trent where the teaching of the church was given superiority and Tradition was given equality to the Scriptures. As we see, the Church Fathers' statements do not agree with Trent's lies.

We could continue with Cyprian, Hippolatus, Eusebius Pamphilus, Athanasias, St. Ambrose, Hilary, Gregory Nyassen, Chrysostrum, and others. All embraced the authority, supremacy and inerrancy of Scripture. It is the only path to the truth of Jesus Christ and therefore the only path to saving faith. Are you not curious as to why the Roman Church through false teaching and black magic sacraments prevents you from coming to your own interpretation of Scripture? Why do you suppose that they demand you believe only what they teach and not what you read? Just who is their master? It is not Christ, it is not God, who is left? Remember the demon-possessed serpent in the garden with Adam and Eve? He turned them away from the Word of God, and thereby brought the whole human race into sin and death when Adam rebelled against that Word.

Think about it. What you have read in this book and what you will read, is incontrovertible proof that the Roman Church is built and sustained by lies. Who is the father of lies?

> Ye are of your father the devil, and the lusts of your father it is your will to do. He was a murderer from the beginning, and standeth not in the truth, because there is no truth in him. When he speaketh a lie, he speaketh of his own: for he is a liar, and the father thereof (John 8:44 ASV).

Does The Roman Church Have Sole Authority For Interpreting Scripture?

[Let no one] wresting the sacred Scripture to his own senses, presume to interpret the said sacred Scripture contrary to that sense which the holy mother Church, whose it is to judge of the true sense and interpretation of the holy Scriptures (*The Sacred & Oecumenical Council of Trent,* Rev. J. Waterworth p. 19).

The Roman Church claims authority in interpreting the Scriptures. However, the Apostle Peter wrote:

> Knowing this first, that no prophecy of scripture is of private interpretation. For no prophecy ever came by the will of man: but men spake from God, being moved by the Holy Spirit (2 Peter 1:20-21 ASV).

There is a question that should occur here. Does the Roman Church possess the Holy Spirit? If so, is the Holy Spirit exclusive to them or can individuals, also have Him?

The purpose of the Roman Church at Trent was to prevent mankind from reading the Bible. They were taught that they were to rely on the church to tell them what the Bible meant. The problem is that few, very few, of the Bishops, Priests, or Deacons ever read the Bible. That was one of the reforms discussed at Trent that did not get reformed.

This claim to exclusive authority of interpretation is "through" the "magisterium" of the Roman Church. What they pronounce as true supposedly is given by the Holy Spirit, whether or not it agrees with Scripture. This as silliness. They have God contradicting Himself. If He does, then He is not God. I think, though, that this may be their goal. They spend a lot of time and ritual contradicting the Word of God, therefore they must be trying to prove that God is not. Sounds like the demon-possessed serpent in the Garden of Eden, does it not?

How about it though? Are the "divines" (theologians) of the church really in agreement on what the Bible says? They would have to be, would they not, if the Holy Spirit is exclusively teaching the Roman Church what the Scriptures have to say. Look at the notes from the *Duoay-Rheims Bible* (Catholic Bible) explaining Revelation 22:10:

> For the time is at hand ...That is, when compared to eternity, all time and temporal things vanish, and are but of short duration. As to the time when the chief predictions should come to pass, we have no certainty, as appears by the, both of the ancient fathers and late interpreters. **Many think** that most things set down from the 4th chapter to the end, will not be fulfilled till a little time before the end of the world. **Others are of opinion,** that a great part of them, and particularly the fall of the wicked Babylon, happened at the destruction of paganism, by the destruction of heathen Rome, and its' persecuting heathen emperors. Of these interpretations, **see Aleazar**, in his long commentary; **see the learned Bossnet, bishop of Meaux,** in his treatise on this Book; and P. Alleman, in his notes on the same Apocalypse, tom. 12, who in his Preface says, that this, in a great measure, may be now looked upon as the opinion followed by the learned men. In fine, others think that St. John's design was in a mystical way, by metaphors and allegories, to represent the attempts and persecutions of the wicked against the servants of God, the punishments that should in a short time fall upon Babylon, that is, upon all the wicked in general: the eternal happiness and reward, which God had reserved for the pious inhabitants of Jerusalem, that is, for his faithful servants, after their short trials and the tribulations of this mortal life. In the mean time we meet with many profitable instructions and admonitions, which we may easily enough understand: but we have no certainty when we apply these predictions to particular events: **for as St. Jerome takes notice,** the Apocalypse has as many mysteries as words, or rather mysteries in every word. *Apocalypsis Joannis tot habet Sacramenta quot verba– parum dixi, in verbis singulis multiplices latent intelligentiae* (Ep. ad Paulin, t. 4. p. 574. Edit. Benedict).

Notice please these words: **different opinions, many think, others of the opinion.** I thought the church had the ability, through the guidance of the Holy Spirit to give clear definitions of what the Bible says. The notes go on to point out that their leading theologians disagree. Perhaps they are the ones that should be excluded from giving interpretations from Scripture because they do not have the guidance of the Holy Spirit that they claim.

You must also consider your responsibility to search the Scriptures. Consider the Berean Church in the Book of Acts:

> And the brethren immediately sent away Paul and Silas by night unto Berea: who when they were come thither went into the synagogue of the Jews. Now these were more noble than those in Thessalonica, in that they received the word with all readiness of the mind, examining the Scriptures daily, whether these things were so. Many of them therefore believed; also of the Greek women of honorable estate, and of men, not a few (Acts 17:10-12 ASV).

If you are a member of the body of Christ you should be searching the Scriptures and reaching out to others with the truth, just like the Bereans. You have a responsibility to read the Scriptures, and to be part of a Church that teaches from the Bible consistently. You have a responsibility to proclaim this word to those you come into contact with.

That is, you have this responsibility **if** you know Jesus Christ as your Savior and Lord, if you have been regenerated. Otherwise, you need to search the Scriptures for the way to salvation.

Jabberwocky and Gobbledegook

"When I use a word," Humpty Dumpty said, in a rather scornful tone, "it means just what I choose it to mean, neither more nor less."

"The question is," said Alice, "whether you can make words mean so many different things."

"The question is," said Humpty Dumpty, "which is to be master—that's all."

Alice was too much puzzled to say anything; so after a minute Humpty Dumpty began again. "They've a temper, some of them—particularly verbs; they're the proudest—adjectives you can do anything with, but not verbs—however, I can manage the whole lot of them! Impenetrability! That's what I say!"

"Would you tell me, please," said Alice, "what that means?"

"Now you talk like a reasonable child," said Humpty Dumpty, looking very much pleased. "I meant by 'impenetrability' that we've had enough of that subject, and it would be just as well if you'd mention what you mean to do next, as I suppose you don't mean to stop here all the rest of your life."

"That's a great deal to make one word mean," Alice said in a thoughtful tone.

"When I make a word do a lot of work like that," said Humpty Dumpty, "I always pay it extra."

"Oh!" said Alice. She was too much puzzled to make any other remark.

—From *Jabberwockey* by Lewis Carrol

While doing the research for this book I have been amazed at the constant "plethora" of words the Roman Church uses to explain [?] its positions. It seems either to talk out of both sides of its mouth or repeat itself so often one would think that many things are said. "Jabberwockey," or perhaps "gobbledegook" is the best way to describe this type of communication. Some of both are in the following statement from Pope Pius IX in 1846.

And that the Most Merciful God may more readily hear our prayers and grant our desires, let us have recourse to the intercession of the Most Holy Mother of God, the Immaculate Virgin Mary, our most sweet mother, our **mediatrix,** our **advocate,** our **Firmest Hope,** the source of our **confidence,** and whose protection is most powerful and most efficacious with God.

—Pope Pius IX at the Church of St. Mary the Greater, November 9, 1846.

In this section we launch into the issues of the worship of Mary, the saints, relics, the Great White Throne Judgement, and the fiction of Purgatory.

The Virgin Mary
or Goddess Myrionymus, (Ishtar) Queen of Heaven, The Woman with a Thousand Names?

Earlier we cited a kidnapping by Pius IX. I thought it would be appropriate to start our consideration of Mary with his words from his encyclical letter referencing her. Consider the labels and activities he applies to Mary.

1. **Intercessor:** the word means mediator.
2. **Mother of God:** nowhere in the Bible is there mention that God had a mother.
3. **Immaculate:** reference to her perpetual virginity (but what about the brothers of Jesus?).
4. **Our mother:** they also label the Roman Church as "mother." How many "mothers" do they have?
5. **Our mediatrix:** the word means intercessor, same thing as #1.
6. **Our advocate:** a person who pleads another person's cause, an intercessor (#1), a mediator (#5).
7. **Our Firmest Hope:** means confidence.

   Really? Our Firmest Hope? In this statement alone, Christ has been replaced as our object of faith. Faith in Christ is clearly taught in Scripture. Nowhere is faith in Mary taught in the Bible.
8. **The source of our confidence:** means hope.

   Again the Roman Church has ascribed to Mary, what is Christ's.
9. **Offers the most effective protection with God:** means confidence. One might ask in this regard, is their god still a threat?

Number 1 and numbers 5 through 9 essentially say the same thing. They claim that Mary is a mediator between God and man. Which one is presenting the truth: the Bible or the Roman Church? Remember Numbers 23:19? It says that "God is not a man that He should lie or the son of man that He should repent." Well, if there are any lies here, they are generated from the Roman Church. Here is what the Bible says about our **one** mediator.

> For there is one God, **one mediator** also between God and men, **himself man**, Christ Jesus, who gave himself a ransom for all; the testimony to be borne in its own times (1 Timothy 2:5-6 ASV).
>
> And to Jesus **the** mediator of a new covenant (Hebrews 12:13 ASV).

Do not these passages eliminate Mary as intercessor, mediator, and advocate? Indeed, the Roman Church catches itself in its own lie. On page 17 of *Vatican Council II (Volume 1)* Christ is called *the mediator*. Also, St. Cyril wrote, "This clearly states **one** mediator" (*Commentary on the Gospel of St. John, Book II* Chapters 11-12).

They say that Mary is **the** mediator on one hand, and that Christ is **the** mediator on the other. You cannot attribute exclusivity of an attribute to more than one person. It makes communication meaningless when you do. The Roman Church's attribution of the role of mediator, intercessor, or advocate to both Mary and Christ is jabberwocky. Further, to assign this attribute to Mary, by the evidence of God's Word as shown above, is clearly a lie.

Here is more proof that the attributions to Mary, as cited above, are jabberwocky. The following was taken from *Catechism of the Catholic Church* published in 1995 by Doubleday.

> *Page 190:* "Only Christ is our confidence." (Remember previously, Mary was cited as "our confidence.").
>
> *Page 190:* "He always makes intercession for us." (Again, a role also assigned to Mary.)
>
> *Page 191:* "Christ intercedes constantly for us." (Do I need to say it? Mary is assigned the role of mediator, intercessor, and advocate by the Roman Church. The Catholic Catechism also assigns these roles although they are really one role as the words mean the same thing.) They are guilty of pure jabberwockey; this is an example of talking out of both sides of one's mouth. The Church at Rome is fostering a lie.

What Did Christ Say About Mary's Role?

Consider what Christ said of Mary in the Bible. His statement defines her importance to salvation and to the state of blessedness of the believer:

> And it came to pass, as he said these things, a certain woman out of the multitude lifted up her voice, and said unto him, Blessed is the womb that bare thee, and the breasts which thou didst suck. But he said, **Yea rather, blessed are they that hear the word of God, and keep it!** (Luke 11:27 ASV).

Christ emphasized the importance of the Word of God over the importance of His mother, Mary. Rather than concentrating on the "blessedness" of Mary, Jesus said we are blessed by hearing the Word and keeping it.

What is Mary's status with Christ? The following verse describes this relationship rather well.

> While he was yet speaking to the multitudes, behold, his mother and his brethren stood without, seeking to speak to him. And one said unto him, Behold, thy mother and thy brethren stand without, seeking to speak to thee. But he answered and said unto him that told him, who is my mother? And who are my brethren? And he stretched forth his hand towards his disciples, and said, Behold, my mother and my brethren! For whosoever shall do the will of my Father who is in heaven, he is my brother, and sister, and mother (Matthew 12:46-50 ASV).

All of those who do the will of the Father, God, have equal status before Him. If you have placed your faith in Christ as your Savior from sin, and made Him, also, your Lord, then you, Mary, and the Lord's brothers (that believed) are all equal. Mary has no special mediatorial status. We all can come to the throne room of God and petition God, Himself, in the name of Christ, who is our sole mediator.

Remember Luke 11:27: "Rather, blessed are they that hear the Word of God and keep it." This has been the problem of sinners since the first Adam. Mankind continually devises ways to create a "religion" apart from God, by rejecting His Word. The first step in blessedness (salvation) is to hear the Word, or read it. Get your Bible out and regularly read it. Find a group that studies and teaches the Word of God and join it. Watch out for frauds, though, Satan has motivated them since the beginning of time.

Mary Myth Manifested

Where and when did the idea of Mary being intercessor, mediatrix, and advocate originate? It appears to have originated in the eighth century from a story written by Paul the Deacon, a monk at Monte Cassino in Italy. The story was titled *The Legend of Theophilus.* The story is a tad farfetched but Theophilus was a real person.

Our hero was named Bishop of Adana, who lived in what is now the country of Turkey. He declined out of humility and was "unfairly" replaced by another. Mr. Theophilus became angry and contacted the Devil, making a contract to serve him. Theophilus soon wised up and knew that he had made a terrible mistake. He fasted and prayed. He particularly prayed to Mary. She interceded and obtained both the absolution of his sin and the return of the contract he had entered into with the Devil. From this one fictional story from the eighth century comes the teaching that Mary is our mediator.

With that story in mind, you might ask where "Mariology" came from. It is also fiction, pure fiction. Here is some "source" information.

> For the facts, themselves, it is necessary, if one wishes to add anything to the gospel narrative, to gather from early Christian literature, evidences of diverse value and not seldom of doubtful value, from which may be adduced, occasionally facts, but more frequently merely conjectures and probabilities. (Page v, Author's Preface, *Saint Mary the Virgin,* Rene-Marie de la Broise. Translated by Harold Gidney; Duckworth and Co., London, 1906).

Mr. de la Broise goes on to categorize three aspects of reaching the truth about Mary.

    1. The historical account of the events of her life.
- The Gospels and other books of Holy Scripture.
- Accounts handed down by the Fathers and early church historians (subject to embellishments, of course).

ESCAPE FROM PAGANISM

- The apocryphal writings (writings that pretend to be Scripture but were rejected as such. They are pure fiction.)
- Personal revelation from the apparitions of certain saints or persons who have died in the odor of sanctity. (More fiction.)

2. It is necessary to give some idea of the mind of Mary and of her inner life. (de la Broise admits this involves a certain amount of conjecture.) This is pure divination! Of course any Tarot Card reader could do it.

> de la Broise states "Yet, he who does not attempt this, neglects an aspect of the subject which is of much greater importance than the question of chronology or of purely material facts."
>
> "To find this information one must study teachings of theologians, the meditations of the saints, who's minds in some degree resemble the mind of Mary and are able to realize and approximate idea of her thoughts and affections."
>
> "The opinion of the Church which, living by the spirit of Jesus, cannot mistake the spirit which animated His mother."

3. The part assigned to Mary in the divine scheme of the incarnation and redemption must be set forth. As "Mother of God" she is associated with all the "mysteries" of the Incarnate Word.

> "If one should be tempted to find exaggeration in all the great things the Fathers of the Church and the saints have said of Mary, it must be called to mind that her motherhood is the source and measure of all her privileges and supremacy.
>
> We can know all of this by the infallible teaching of the Church.
>
> (*Saint Mary, the Virgin;* by de la Broise, p. viii-ix).

Then, in speaking of the parents' of Mary, here is the source of our information according to Bishop Ullathorne:

> A celebrated divine has made the remark that, though some persons wonder that the Evangelists are silent on the parents of the Blessed Virgin, and have left tradition to record what we know respecting them, yet was this arranged with an especial design by the providence of God. (*The Immaculate Conception of the Mother of God,* by The Right Rev. Bishop Ullathorne; Richardson and Son, London, 1865. p. 105).

Tradition! We can know these things through tradition! One can see why the "divines" at the Council of Trent fought so hard to have Tradition and the Pope's Words on par with the Scriptures. Without Tradition and the Pope's word (the infallible teaching of the Church) their whole system folds.

Mary, Mother Of God

In the early fifth century a dispute arose between the eastern churches and Rome over the issue of Mary being the Mother of God. The chief disputants were Nestorius for the east and Cyril for Rome. This council was held in Ephesus in 431 AD.

Nestorius resisted the idea that Mary was the Mother of God. In doing this, though, he separated Christ into two natures: one God and one man. Instead of Christ being one, wholly God and wholly man.

His opponent was a man named Cyril, now a "Saint" of the Roman Church. Cyril held that "since the Word became flesh" (John 1:14) that when Jesus was born as the God/Man, Mary was mother of the whole person, therefore the mother of God.

Cyril believed that you could not separate the two and talk only about the divinity of Christ, or only about the humanity of Christ. The two natures were unified and inseparable. The majority of the participants at the Council of Ephesus agreed with Cyril and condemned the belief of Nestorius. The position on Mary as Mother of God, then, was not "legitimized" until 431 years after Christ was resurrected from the dead.

You might ask: "Since Christ was fully both man and God, how can you maintain that Mary was only mother of the man and not also of God?"

Well, if the unity of the God/Man cannot be separated, neither can the unity of the Godhead. Our God is Triune. God is one, but three persons, Father, Son, and Holy Spirit. The three persons are of one essence. One essence means one existence, one "stuff," or one substance. You cannot separate one person of the Godhead from another. So to claim that Mary is the mother of God is to claim that she is the mother not only of the Son of God, but also of the Father and Holy Spirit. Mary is not the mother of God, queen of heaven or any of that nonsense. She is the mother of the humanity of Christ.

The question: "Since Jesus Christ is fully God and fully man and born of Mary, how is she not also the mother of God if she is the mother of Christ's humanity?" is difficult to answer. One cannot separate the divinity from the humanity of Christ, that is true. Also true, however, is the fact that the only thing Mary could pass on to her son was humanity, she was not and is not a goddess, therefore could not pass a divine nature.

Suppose a woman and her husband wanted a baby, but the woman's health was such that she would not survive the pregnancy. So a surrogate mother was sought and engaged. The doctor, in his laboratory, took the man's sperm and fertilized the woman's egg, then implanted it in the surrogate mother. Nine months later the child is born. Who is the mother? From whom come the genes? The surrogate mother only provided the nurturing and the growing space for the pregnancy term. All of the baby's characteristics came from its biological parents. The people who supplied the genes are the biological parents. The biological mother is the one that supplied the egg. However, the biological parents cannot and do not pass on to the child attributes that they do not possess. This is a similar situation with Mary; she did not possess divinity and therefore could not pass it on. Further, the child in her womb was God before He entered her womb. His divinity has no "mother."

How can this be? God has not spoken on this point. The answer has not been revealed to us. Any conjecture or supposed facts are pure meta-physics. Remember what that means? It is an area which our reason, our senses cannot define for us. To attempt to explain situations for which the facts have not been revealed to us, is non-sensual, because the facts needed for the answers are non-sensible. Our "senses" cannot ascertain the data needed to draw a conclusion. My prognostications are no better than those of anyone else. Just because it "seems right" does not make it right.

Many substitute their imaginations for fact and profess as true that which cannot be known except by the revelation of God. Many do not care that God has not spoken to the issue.

Imagination goes by several terms such as **Tradition, Visions, Dreams,** and **Church Teaching.** Remember the penalty for adding to the Word of God, which God has pronounced as complete for now? Let's look at that verse again.

> I testify unto every man that heareth the words of the prophecy of this book, if any man shall add unto them, God shall add unto him the plagues which are written in this book (Revelations 22:18 ASV).

Consider this;

> And Zacharias was troubled when he saw him, and fear fell upon him. But the angel said unto him, Fear not, Zacharias: because thy supplication is heard, and thy wife Elisabeth shall bear thee a son, and thou shalt call his name John. And thou shalt have joy and gladness; and many shall rejoice at his birth. For he shall be great in the sight of the Lord, and he shall drink no wine nor strong drink; and he shall be filled with the Holy Spirit, even from his mother's womb (Luke 1:12-15 ASV).

Since the prophet John the Baptist was "filled with the Holy Spirit from his mother's womb" this means that when John the Baptist was born, the Holy Spirit (who is God the Spirit) was part of him. Does this make Elisabeth, his mother, the Mother of God also? The rational that the Church of Rome applies to Mary about being the mother of God because she birthed the God/Man fits here also, so, is there, in fact, two mothers of God? Now I am not saying that John the Baptist was fully God and fully man as was Christ, only that the Spirit of God filled him at his birth. John's birth, though, has enough similarity with Christ's that my question is legitimate.

Mary Queen of Heaven

Escape From Paganism

From the teaching that Mary is the mother of God, the Roman Church pulls the concept that she is also the Queen of Heaven. Really? Is this where they got it from? It really came from somewhere else. Consider the following prayer to the Queen of Heaven.

> *"O royal_____, of majestic mein,*
> *Aerial formed, divine, _____ blessed queen,*
> *Throned in the bosom of heavenly air,*
> *The race of mortels is thy constant care;*
> *The cooling gales of thy power alone inspires,*
> *Which nourish life, which every life desires;*
> *Mother of showers and winds, from thee alone*
> *Producing all things, mortal life is known;*
> *All natures show thy temperament divine,*
> *And universal sway alone is thine,*
> *With sounding blasts of wind, the swelling rea*
> *And rolling rivers roar when shook by thee.*
>
> –Quoted from *Taylors "Orphic Hymns" in Tale of Two Babylons;* Rev. Alexander Hislop 1916

This could have been written in adoration of Mary. Many things that the Church of Rome does write of her are equally grandiose. So who was it written to? Fill in the first blank with the name Juno, and the second blank with the name Jove, or Jove's. Juno, as the wife of Jove, the major god of the pantheon, is the Queen of Heaven. Juno was also called Astarte, Minerva, Venus, Athena, Diana of Ephesus, and other names for the Queen of Heaven used by pagans throughout the world. In the Hindu religion today, the "Queen of Heaven" is known as "Kali;" in pagan Buddhism, the Queen's name is Kuan Yin. In the Bible, the Book of Revelation identifies this woman (the Queen of Heaven) as:

And the woman was arrayed in purple and scarlet, and decked with gold and precious stone and pearls, having in her hand a golden cup full of abominations, even the unclean things of her fornication, and upon her forehead a name written, MYSTERY, BABYLON THE GREAT, THE MOTHER OF THE HARLOTS AND OF THE ABOMINATIONS OF THE EARTH (Revelation 17:4-5 ASV).

To label Mary as the mother of God, or Queen of Heaven is jabberwocky although, the Mary that the Roman Church describes **does** fit the description of the pagan's Queen of Heaven. It seems to me that there is a connection. That connection is reinforced by the similarities of the pagan's veneration of the Queen of Heaven and the liturgy and veneration of Mary by the Roman Church.

The Fable Continues

"**G**od" says St. Epiphanus, "prepared for His Only-Begotten Son, the heavenly bride, a Virgin, whom the Father loved, whom the Son inhabited, whom the Holy Ghost searched thoroughly" (*The Immaculate Conception of The Mother of God* by The Right Rev. Bishop Ullathorne, D.D. 1855. p. 8).

> We have now to consider what foundations God laid when He created Mary; when He framed her for an office which raised her so far above the laws and customs of our human nature. We have to consider how the Most High did found His tabernacle. We have to consider, how the Eternal Word, in the infinity of His power, prepared a mother for Himself. We have to consider how the Holy Spirit of grace prepared His spouse (ibid, p. 13).
>
> To His true dove, His one true spouse, the Holy Spirit sings that Canticle: "One is my dove, my perfect one is but one, the only one of her mother, the chosen of her that bore her" (ibid, p. 114).
>
> Who is immaculate, who is the Spouse of the Eternal Wisdom, and the Mother of the King of our Salvation (ibid, p. 1150.

Here the claim is made that Mary was married to God the Father, or is it the Holy Spirit? It could not be the Son as that would be incest. The quotes are three for one in favor of the Holy Spirit being married to Mary. What I really think, though, is that this is just another example of jabberwockey.

There are three concepts of love in the Greek language: agape, philos, and eros. Agape is a doing love, a normal love, a charitable love. Philos is brotherly love. Eros is a sexual love.

One wonders which word Mr. Epiphanus used. It is obvious that he is stating that God the Father's love was more for Mary than other women. This love is also connected to the conception of the God/Man, Christ Jesus. Could God be subject to erotic emotions? What Epiphanus states seem to indicate this. The claim is pure hokum, which means, well, let's put it down as silliness. To ascribe to God the emotion of "eros" would make

God subject to lust and therefore subject to sin. The Roman Church, again, is guilty of an **abomination** in teaching this. When you get to page 353 you will see that the pagans had a similar, but incestuous love relationship amongst the gods.

Well, you might think that I would be at an end to this, but I'm **not!** The Roman Church has the credulity to teach that Christ made His "offering" in that pure Temple of Mary.

> "Coming into this world He said: A body Thou hast fitted to me, Holocausts for sin did not please Thee. Behold I come. In the head of the book it is written of me: that I should do Thy will, O God." And Mary was that most pure Temple in which the great High Priest made His offering (ibid P. 9).

This is an outrage! Christ made His offering in the womb of Mary? This teaching throws out the cross and Christ's atoning death. They cannot believe this! This has to be more jabberwockey.

The Immaculate Conception

The immaculate conception is simply the belief that Mary was born without original sin. This would mean that she was without a sin nature. This belief was not officially adopted by the Roman Church until 1476 when the feast of the Immaculate Conception was authorized by Pope Sixtus IV. Then in the Council of Trent (1545 to 1563) she was specifically excluded from the decree on the universality of original sin. (See *Catholicism* by Richard P. Mc Brien, P. 1092.)

> "As regards the Blessed Virgin, the Council does not intend to define anything: although it is piously believed that she was conceived without original sin." This opinion had a majority in its favor, but was opposed by all the bishops of the Dominican order, and by a few other prelates (*Council of Trent,* Rev. J. Waterworth, Catholic Publication Society, New York. P. XCVI).

By the 1560s, the immaculate conception of Mary, while now official Roman Church doctrine, was still controversial and without unanimous embrace within that organization.

The problem the Roman Church was trying to solve was that of the passage of original sin to our Savior, Jesus Christ. To be the second Adam, He had to be born without a sin nature. If Mary could be immaculate, then Christ, born of her, would be without the sin nature possessed by all mankind.

What the Roman Church did not understand is that the sin nature is passed down by the men. I do not mean to say that women are not possessed of it; just that the passage of original sin from generation to generation is from the man. So?

There are two genealogies of Christ in the New Testament. One genealogy is in Matthew chapter 1, and the other in Luke chapter 3. The one in Mathew established Christ's legal right to the throne of David, which He will occupy at His return. The other established His ancestry all the way back to Adam, the son of God.

The Luke lineage is that of Mary. Heli, or Eli, depending on the Bible version you are reading, was Mary's father. Yes, I know, the Roman Church teaches that her parents were the fictional Joachim and Anna, both now sainted by the Romans. They did not exist!

"Wait up there," you might exclaim, "My Bible says that Heli (Eli) was the father of Joseph."

Let's look at the passage closely.

> And Jesus himself, when he began to teach, was about thirty years of age, being the son (as was supposed) of Joseph, the son of Heli (Luke 3:23 ASV).

Understand that the original text was written in Greek and that the Greek language had no punctuation. The brackets, commas, periods and such are the product of our translators. This is an important point, which we will return to. For now, note that this verse seems to indicate Heli is the father of Joseph. Now let's look at Matthew's genealogy:

> And **Jacob** begat Joseph the husband of Mary, of whom was born Jesus, who is called Christ (Matthew 1:16 ASV).

Now Joseph could not have had two fathers, so is the Bible contradicting itself? No, Joseph did not have two fathers, nor is the Bible contradicting itself. Our translators goofed! Let's go back to Luke 3:23 and change the location of some punctuation marks.

> And Jesus himself, when he began to teach, was about thirty years of age (being the son as was supposed of Joseph) the son of Heli.

Punctuated this way, the verse not only eliminates Joseph as the biological father, it also eliminates Heli as the biological father of Joseph, and connects Jesus with Heli as his maternal grandfather, the father of Mary. We see that an "apparent" biblical contradiction is cleared up.

It also solves the issue of the passage of original sin to Christ. His mother, like all women, could not and did not pass it, even though she had a sin nature just like the rest of us. The sin nature is passed down by man. If you will recall, God told the

Serpent, in Genesis 3, that the Seed of the women would crush his head. Jesus is the Seed that God promised and He is the Seed without a sin nature.

For an excellent discussion of this, I refer you to the book *A Harmony of the Gospels* by A.T. Robertson D.D., LLD, Litt.D. The discussion is published in Note 5, page 259-262 in the section titled **Notes on Special Points.** This book may be downloaded from www.archive.org for free. It is an excellent resource, I recommend getting it.

Mary was born with a sin nature. She was a sinner just like you and me. The Bible is clear on this point in both the Old and New Testaments:

> As it is written, There is none righteous, no, not one; There is none that understandeth, There is none that seeketh after God; They have all turned aside, they are together become unprofitable; There is none that doeth good, no, not, so much as one (Romans 3:10-12 ASV).
>
> There is none that doeth good. Jehovah looked down from heaven upon the children of men, To see if there were any that did understand, That did seek after God. They are all gone aside; they are together become filthy; There is none that doeth good, no, not one (Psalm 14:1-3 ASV).

Mary was included in this group of creatures God defines as "filthy," just as you and I are. Mary was saved by her faith in the Lord, His Word, and justified by His death upon the cross in the same way that all believers are saved and justified. Further, she was sanctified by the Holy Spirit, a just person, made perfect–just as all believers are or are in the process of becoming.

The Roman Church claims many apparitions of Mary over the centuries. For example, more than 2,000 apparitions of Mary are claimed for Garabandal, Spain, between the years 1961 and 1965. The vast majority of the "teachings" about Mary come from this type of mysticism. Either it is information garnered from these "appearances," from the apparitions of saints, or just plain conjecture (see *The Saints; Saint Mary the Virgin,* Rene-Marie de La Broise, pages 220-225.) Mr. de La Broise presents admitted conjecture as fact. This is a habitual tactic I see used by Roman Church writers.

Mary, the Perpetual Virgin

The position of the Roman Church is that Mary never had sexual relations with any man. This means that she never "knew" (in the biblical sense) her husband, Joseph. This is rebellion against the purpose of God for marriage. It is asserted that the only child she ever bore was Jesus. What is the truth? Jesus had brothers and sisters; that is the plain reading of Scripture. To say that He did not is either to lie, or to make God a liar.

> Is not this the carpenter, the son of Mary, and brother of James, and Joses, and Judas, and Simon? and are not his sisters here with us? And they were offended in him. And Jesus said unto them, A prophet is not without honor, save in his own country, and among his own kin, and in his own house (Mark 6:3 ASV).

No more needs to be said here. In Scripture, brother and sister means brother and sister! Doesn't that astound you? Brother and sister do not mean cousin or aunt or uncle or best friend. Brother and sister mean brother and sister. Hard to believe I know, but it is true! Roman Church dogma perverts the Scripture to force brother and sister to mean cousins. This is similar to making the automobile a grasshopper!

You accuse me of sarcasm? You can, because it fits. I am sarcastic against liars. The Roman Church has for centuries fostered this lie along with many others. My sarcasm is mild compared to the judgment that will be assessed against such liars at the Great White Throne Judgment levied by Christ Himself.

A Wild West Story, Well, Almost.
The Death and Assumption of Mary

On page 223 of his book, Mr. de la Broise makes this remarkable statement:

> Holy Scripture says nothing of the life led by the mother of Jesus in that retreat (allegedly living in Jerusalem with the family of John) nor of the influence which she exercised on those around her. God seems to have willed that we should only be able to guess at much concerning the great mystery which encompassed Mary (ibid).

Now just why do you suppose God did this? Was He being mean or did He have a purpose? Do you suppose that He had other things He wanted us to do and concentrate on? Is it not that what He has spoken is spoken for our instruction and what He has not spoken is not important for our salvation, sanctification, or service to Him? Is this not so? Was this not a lesson to be learned from Adam's rebellion? Is it not time to sober up and pay attention to what He has said and forget the imaginings of unbelieving "theologians" and "sacerdotal" liars?

The "legend" also says that Mary was raised by the priests at the Temple in Jerusalem. It says that her parents dedicated her to God and left her there. Was she not, then, the original nun? This is **nunsence.**

Is the word "liar" too strong or would you object that it is unsupported? Let's look at what is said about the circumstances of Mary's death. I will quote from *The Saints, Saint Mary the Virgin* by de la Broise, beginning on page 247. Referring to the details of Mary's death:

> "The details vary very much, according to the different texts and their various editions. After an angel, carrying a palm branch, had come to announce to Mary her coming deliverance, the apostles suddenly assembled round her – brought miraculously upon the clouds of the sky – say a large number of texts. In the midst of the band of disciples and holy women, Christ himself appeared, surrounded by a multitude of angels. In accordance with Mary's own request, He promised that at all times and in all places, whosoever should pray to her and make a request in her name should find grace and mercy with God. The virgin

blessed the faithful, who honoured her as their mother, and she committed her soul to Jesus.

Hold it right here! There is no reason to proceed further with Mary's demise as there are enough lies told here to make Adam's sin look like an act of innocence. What are the lies? I will not deal with all of them, only the ones that seem to make God a liar in what He has spoken.

Did you notice? The apostles arrived at this pre-death wake riding on the clouds. Yuppers, they came there through the friendly skies of United.

Christ, Himself, appeared! This is to claim that Christ returned to earth. What does God's Word say about this?

> And when he had said these things, as they were looking, he was taken up; and a cloud received him out of their sight. And while they were looking steadfastly into heaven as he went, behold, two men stood by them in white apparel; who also said, Ye men of Galilee, why stand ye looking into heaven? This Jesus, who was received up from you into heaven shall so come in like manner as ye beheld him going into heaven (Acts 1:9-11 ASV).

This Scripture is referring to the second coming of Christ. In the "story" about Mary, Christ came to the pre-death "wake" of Mary. This would mean His second coming has already occurred. Clearly it is a lie, as when He comes the second time it will be in power and majesty and His Messiah-ship begins. He will set upon the Throne of David and rule the earth. So, this, alone, proves that the above story is a lie.

> "In accordance with Mary's own request, He promised that at all times and in all places, whosoever should pray to her and make a request in her name should find grace and mercy with God."

This is a horrible statement. It is the devil at work, ensnaring people by a lie that will be, for them, a cause of dwelling eternally with him in the Lake of Fire. This statement makes Mary the cause of salvation. Do you want the mercy and grace of God to apply to your account? Pray to Mary is what this says. It is a damnable statement. It is frightening to consider the hundreds of thousands who will be forever in hell because they believed and practiced this lie.

What is the truth?

> God determined in eternity past, to whom His Mercy and Grace would apply. "Blessed be the God and Father of our Lord Jesus Christ, who hath blessed us with every spiritual blessing in the heavenly places in Christ: even as he chose us in him before the foundation of the world, that we should be holy and without blemish before him in love: having foreordained us unto adoption as sons through Jesus Christ unto himself" (Ephesians 1:3-5 ASV).
>
> And Jehovah said unto Moses, I will do this thing also that thou hast spoken; for thou hast found favor in my sight, and I know thee by name. And he said, Show me, I pray thee, thy glory. And he said, I will make all my goodness pass before thee, and will proclaim the name of Jehovah before thee; and I will be gracious to whom I will be gracious, and will show mercy on whom I will show mercy (Exodus 33:17-19 ASV).

Election is the issue in the Ephesians' passage. God chose those to receive His mercy and grace in eternity past. Prayers to Mary in this regard are therefore pointless and an abomination. Notice also that those who are "foreordained" to adoption as sons are so ordained through Jesus Christ unto Himself. Mary is neither mentioned nor intended. Therefore, Mr. de la Broise has written a lie.

Going onto the Exodus passage, we see God telling Moses that He will exercise His grace and mercy upon whomever **He** wills! Is God being imperious? What, in the name of justice, gives Him this right? Let's look at Romans 3:25-26 (ASV):

> whom God set forth to be a propitiation, through faith, in his blood, to show his righteousness because of the passing over of the sins done aforetime, in the forbearance of God; for the showing, I say, of his righteousness at this present season: that he might himself be just, and the justifier of him that hath faith in Jesus.

The sacrifice of Jesus Christ, the God/Man, upon the cross, is the righteousness or justice of God that enables God to determine on whom He will exercise His grace and mercy. Mary is **not** involved in this. Again, prayers to Mary for God's mercy and grace are an abomination. Our prayers must be to our mediator, Christ. These prayers will be ineffectual and also an abomination unless we have placed our faith in Him, and Him alone, as our Savior.

Well, I have never been to a pre-death wake, but this one must have been a lulu! Observe that not only is Christ there with a crowd of angels, and the disciples are wafted in, riding on clouds, but "numberless miracles are performed to punish the perverse Jews."

Can't you see it? Miracles going off like fireworks and the perverse Jews hopping and skipping around, screaming and yelling because of the punishment they are receiving from the miracles. Reminds me of a drunken gunman in the old west, shooting at some dude's feet making him dance! This wake is a real humdinger of a celebration. Numberless miracles were performed indeed. This stuff is pure jabberwocky.

Mr. de la Broise is truly remarkable. He writes imaginative things as fact, then admits to the use of fiction, but claims that such fiction embodies true facts. Here is a sample from his book:

> Who shall say where history ends and where legendary additions commence? In any case, however legendary and uncertain a great part of it may be, we may be sure that a foundation of historic truth lies hidden under these ancient narratives and a foundation of theological truth also (Ibid, page 248).

Mary's Dominion in Heaven, or is it Domineering Heaven?

The whole doctrine of Mary, Mother of God, and Queen of Heaven is built upon fiction and, as we have seen, is outright at variance with God's Word. "Mariology" is an abomination towards the living God.

The Assumption of Mary is the "legend" of her bodily resurrection into heaven. Rene de la Broise states:

> "Mary is exalted, leaning upon her well-beloved, for from Him alone she has received her grace, her merit, all her greatness; inseparable from Him in the divine though she is exalted with Him, gently drawn by Him.... He crowned her in the presence of His saints and angels. -He crowned her with all His majesty as King. -Not with one of those crowns reserved for His most faithful servants, but with a crown of royalty (ibid, pages 254-256).

Here is a listing of some of the claims made for Mary's exalted position in heaven by de la Broise (ibid, pages 257-260):

1. She has joint dominion with Christ over all creation.
2. The angels reverence the "supreme" dignity of the Mother of their God.
3. Since they, "probably," have received grace and glory through Christ, they honor her as their mother, her who gave Christ to them.
4. The saints and angels contemplate Mary,
    - a more brilliant radiance of majesty.
    - a new splendor of beauty.
    - a hitherto unknown purging for the sovereign goodness.
    - all of them, they love the supreme love.
5. She united the whole worship of heaven.
6. The mother of Jesus is the chief member, the queen, the mother, the ideal type of the church.
7. She is **united** with the divinity.

8. The church is dependent upon Mary.
9. She is the heavenly mediatrix.
10. She presides with Jesus.
11. She has a rank superior to the whole church triumphant.
12. Our knowledge of Jesus would be insufficient unless we know Mary well.
13. Seen in heaven as the **Redemptress** of our race.
14. She is the head crusher of Satan.
15. Three wills are united in heaven: God the Father, God the Son, and Mary.
16. Our acts of reverence and invocation connect us with God and the Holy Virgin.

It is clear from this list of things that the Roman Church has stolen a page from the religious practices of Pagan Rome. How so? They have deified Mary, transformed her into a goddess. Just look at what is said. We will work backwards through the list.

- **#16, #15, #7:** Three united wills and worship connects us to God and Mary.

United: the word means to become **one.** According to the Roman Church, God and Mary are **one.** When we worship, we are connected to both God and goddess, according to this teaching.

- **#5:** Mary united the whole worship of heaven. You have to pay attention to what is being said. The only inference one can get from this, other than the "feel good about Mary" psychology that is used, is that the worship of God in heaven was pretty disorganized before she got there. God must have been deficient. This statement makes God less than omniscient and omnipotent. In fact, it makes Him less than God.

- **#13:** Mary is **the** Redemptress of our race; she has displaced Christ as the redeemer.

The term "the" is singular, meaning there is only **one.** This is a Roman Church lie, and like the rest of the "stuff" in the list above is pure jabberwocky. It should be derided with the utmost scorn.

Mary did not die for us! To be redeemer, one would have to die for the rest of us. This is the scriptural imperative. Mary did not die for our sin, or sins. It was Christ and Christ alone.

> The wages of sin is death (Romans 6:23). For as by one man sin entered the world and death by sin, so death passed to all men for all have sinned (Romans 5:12). But not as the trespass, so also is the free gift. For if by the trespass of the one the many died, much more did the grace of God, and the gift by the grace of the one man, Jesus Christ, abound unto the many (Romans 5:15).

• **#10, #2, #1:** Mary presides with Jesus, has joint dominon with Christ over all creation and is worshiped by angels.

Jabberwocky, poppycock, filthy lies, rebellion against the living God; **a return to paganism** is how I would describe this.

Christ has all rule, power and authority today. He is reconciling all things.

> Christ, when he raised him from the dead, and made him to sit at his right hand in the heavenly places, far above all rule, and authority, and power, and dominion, and every name that is named, not only in this world, but also in that which is to come: and he put all things in subjection under his feet, and gave him to be head over all things to the church (Ephesians 1:20-22 ASV).

Nothing at all is stated in Scripture about Mary having joint dominion with Christ. The Roman Church is guilty of adding to God's Word. That is outright rebellion against God, just as was Adam in His sin.

Remember the prophecy about the Seed of a woman? The Seed would crush the head of Satan, after he had bruised the heal of the Seed (see Genesis 3:16). That Seed is Christ. Satan bruised His heal on the cross. Christ, though, rose from the dead and

Satan is a defeated foe – his head crushed! Notice #14, the Roman Church claims that Mary did this. Again, not only is this jabberwocky, but rebellion against the living God by changing His Word.

The Mary that Rome talks about is not the Mary of the Bible or Mary the mother of Christ. The Mary they are promoting is the woman with a thousand names. The Mary they reference is the goddess of many pagan religions, you will recognize some of the names, Venus, Minerva, Juno, Ishtar, Astarte, Isis, Diana, and Kali, are just a few of those names.

The Roman Church is **not** Christian; it never was Christian, it is pagan. If you would like to see a tabulation of all the pagan rituals adopted by the Roman Church, there is an excellent, short book at www.archive.org entitled *A Letter from Rome* by Conyers Middleton. It is a free download and I recommend it. It will sustain the point that I have made, that the Roman Church is pagan and not Christian.

The woman who called out, "Blessed is the womb that bare thee, and the breasts which thou did suck" was answered by Jesus, "Yea rather, blessed are they that hear the word of God, and keep it" (Luke 11:27). Jesus, Himself, said that all who do the will of the Father are His brothers, mother and sisters (see Matthew 12:46-50). The Roman Church has perverted the message of Christ, and is responsible for many who will be condemned to the Lake of Fire for an eternity of suffering.

Mary's Little Godlets, the Saints

I **am calling this section** "Mary's Little Godlets," because, as we have seen, it is taught that Mary organized heaven's worship. That would mean that she whipped these godlets into line to properly worship God. Why do I use the term "godlets?" Read on and you will see this substantiated.

"The Invocation, Veneration, and Relics of Saints and on Sacred Images." This is how the subject is introduced in the book *The Sacred and Ecumenical Council of Trent* by Rev. J. Waterworth. What did the Sacred and Ecumenical Council of Trent have to say? Following are their statements (pages 233-234):

- Since from primitive times of the Christian religion and agreeably with the consent of the holy fathers, and the decrees of the councils, they especially instruct the faithful diligently concerning the intercession and invocation of the saints; the honour paid to relics; and the legitimate use of images:

- Teaching that the saints, who reign together with Christ, offer up their own prayers to God for men.

- Invoking the saints can help obtain benefits from God.

- God's son, Jesus Christ is our alone Redeemer and Savior.

- Veneration of the saints is not opposed to the "honour" of the one mediator of God and men, Christ Jesus.

- The holy bodies of the martyrs, and others now living with Christ, and the Temple of the Holy Ghost and which are by Him to be raised unto eternal life, and to be glorified – are to be venerated by the faithful, through which (bodies) benefits are bestowed by God on men.

- They who affirm that veneration and honour are not due to the relics of saints; or that these and other sacred monuments are uselessly honoured by the faithful; and that the places dedicated to the memories of the saints are in vain visited with the view of obtaining their aid; are wholly to be condemned, as the church has already long since condemned and now also condemns them.

What you see above is an example of **gobbledygook** *and* more jabberwocky. This is a lot of circumlocution and rhetoric. Let's examine the material.

The first bulleted point simply states that none of this has the blessing of God because it is not scriptural. Where does it say this? They are claiming Tradition and Church Teaching as the source of the dogma, not Scripture. That is why it qualifies as gobbledygook.

In the second point, though, we get into heresy. They are claiming for the saints the same thing that was claimed for Mary, that they reign with Christ. This is a lie. Scripture clearly tells us that all things have been given to Christ for His dominion.

> far above all rule, and authority, and power, and dominion, and every name that is named, not only in this world, but also in that which is to come: and he put all things in subjection under his feet (Ephesians 1:21-22 ASV).

When Christ returns to earth and begins His millennial reign on earth, the "saints" will rule, in a servant capacity, with Him upon the earth. These saints will be all of the sanctified believers that were members of the true Church.

Consider these five things that God did for Christ (*Dake's Annotated Reference Bible,* Page 213):

- Raised Him from the dead (Ephesians 1:20, 1 Corinthians 15:1-23).
- Exalted Him at His own right hand (Ephesians 1:20, Psalms 110:1, Matthew 26:64).
- Gave Him authority over all powers, good and evil (Ephesians 1:21, 3:10, 6:12, Romans 8:38).
- Gave Him a name above every name, except God the Father (Ephesians 1:21, 1 Corinthians 11:3).
- Put all things in subjection under His feet (Ephesians 1:22, Colossians 1:16-18).

When you consider this, the idea that the "saints" reign with Him is gobbledygook. This is also jabberwocky because, as you recall, the same thing is claimed for their self-created goddess, Mary. Words are really meaningless to these people.

Now we come to the idea of "invoking" the saints to obtain benefits from God. "Invoke" means to call upon, or pray to. In this case it is praying to the saints.

In my research I have seen that this is a central issue of the Roman Church – that of obtaining benefits from God. You do not find much about service to Him, but if you are a believer that is your purpose. When you place your faith in Christ as your Savior and Lord, you become a "doulos," which is the Greek word for "servant." The whole purpose of your salvation is to serve Him, rather than constantly, or only, seeking "benefits." This is not to say that you cannot ask God for help in your times of trouble, but you can go directly to Him. You need not, should not, and cannot, detour through a supposed saint or goddess, Mary.

Woops, look at the one that states "God's Son, Jesus Christ, is our alone Redeemer and Savior." Yes, that is what the book says "our alone Redeemer and Savior." Remember the Roman Church also claims Mary is "Co-redeemer." Christ cannot be the "alone" Redeemer and have a Co-redeemer. The concept is nonsense. The Roman Church tells so many lies it cannot keep them straight; the lies keep catching up with them.

Well the next two are something. The Roman Church states that neither the saints nor their relics (bodies, bones, personal paraphernalia) are to be worshipped, only **venerated.** To venerate means to worship; look it up in your dictionary. For all those, who like me, know this stuff to be false, the Council of Trent condemns us; this means damns to hell! From what I read in Scripture, somebody is going to be surprised. Well, just another example of gobbledygook and jabberwocky.

Shrouded in Fantasy

One might spend a lot of space writing about the phony collections of "relics" and their sale. Things like horse and dog bones representing the bones of saints and being sold to the "faithful" as protection for their lives, or charms of saints to be worn or draped over the car's rearview mirror to protect you while you travel. We could, at long length, consider the silliness of testing the DNA on the Shroud of Turin to see if the image thereon is really that of Jesus.

What is the Shroud of Turin? It is claimed to be a burial cloth. It is widely believed that it is the burial cloth used on Christ. There has been a lot of "science" practiced on this cloth to prove that it is Christ's burial shroud. The Roman Church has been backing this activity, probably because it makes them a lot of money.

Is not the infallible church, though, committing another "fallible?" Why do I ask? I ask because there is another shroud that has been accepted as the burial shroud of Christ, centuries ago.

> The Diocese of Perigueux has a remarkable relic: Pierre Raoul or Gerard, a parish priest in Perigord, brought back, after the First Crusade, the Holy Shroud of Christ, entrusted to him by a dying ecclesiastic of Le Puy, who himself obtained this relic from the legate Adhemar de Monteil (*The Catholic Encyclopedia* Volume XI by Ceorges Goyau, Published 1911, New York).

This is all silliness! Anyone that believes this stuff should sit down, put their head between their knees, take deep breaths and come back to reality.

Some Absolutely Incredible Saints

Saint Oreste

Saint Oreste began life as Mount Soracke, a mountain near Rome. It happened by a corruption of its name into S Oracke (a space between the S and O), then to S. Oreste, which was thought to be the name of a saint. Since the Italians usually wrote the word saint as an "S" in front of the name of the "saint," one can see how this happened. Now the mountain has a Roman Church patron, which is interesting, as the mountain used to have a patron under the pagan system named Apollo.

Saint Amphibolus

This saint is English. As the story goes, he was a disciple of the martyr, St. Albans. Saint Amphibolus, too, was supposedly martyred. Bishop Usher, a noted Bible scholar and historian, gives good evidence that Amphibolus was really the cloak that Albans had on when he was executed. The word amphibolous means "rough and shaggy cloak." Such a cloak was in common usage by the monks in the age of St. Albans. Now, in addition to St. Mountain, we have a St. Cloak.

Saint Veronica

It is alleged that two handkerchiefs in Rome bear a genuine image of Christ. One was sent by Christ to the prince of Edessa, after that prince had written to Christ wanting a picture of Him. The other was given by Christ to a holy woman named Veronica at the time of His execution. His image was imprinted upon the handkerchief she gave to Christ, to wipe His face. These handkerchiefs were, and may still be kept at St. Sylvester's and St. Peter's Church, both in Rome. It turns out that Veronica means "vera," "icon" or "true image." So St. Veronica is really St. Handkerchief.

Think of it: St. Mountain, St. Cloak, and St. Handkerchief. Believe me, we could go on!

Saint Dominic

The Dominican Order was established after St. Dominic, who also promoted the Inquisition. Dominic lived toward the end of the 12th century and into the first part of the 13th century. The following quotes are from John Dowling, D.D., *History of Romanism*, page 325:

> Let the reader have patience to peruse a few of these tales, not copied from protestant, and therefore suspect authors, but from the Dominican historians themselves, and every one of them authorized by the Inquisition.
>
> These disciples of Dominic relate that the mother of their master dreamed that she brought forth a dog, holding a burning torch in his mouth, wherewith he fired the world. Earthquakes and meteors announced his nativity to the earth and the air, and two or three suns and moons extraordinary were hung out for an illumination in heaven. The Virgin Mary received him in her arms as he sprang to birth. When a *sucking babe,* he regularly observed fast days, and would get out of bed and lie upon the ground as a penance. His manhood was as portentous as his infancy. He fed multitudes miraculously, and performed the miracle of Cana with great success. Once, when he fell in with a troop of pilgrims, of different countries, the curse which had been inflicted at Babel (different languages) was suspended for him, and all were enabled to speak one language.

It seems to me that the fabricator, or inventor of Dominic's miracles was trying to make him into a god, as the miracle at Cana, and feeding of the multitudes, were works performed by God the Father through Jesus Christ, who is God the Son.

Well, we will end the fantastic saints recitation here. You can find more of these frauds in two books: Middleton's *Letter from Rome,* and *History of Romanism* by John Dowling D.D. Keep in mind that the Roman Church claims to be infallible.

The Godlets

Augustine of Hippo

This man, sainted by the Roman Church, lived from 354 to 430 AD. He was a Bishop of the Roman Church in North Africa. I am not sure he would have approved of his being "sainted" by the Romans, but, who knows. Of patron saints, I am sure he would have disapproved. Why am I so sure? Augustine was a prolific writer and also a theologian. One of the books he wrote was *The City of God.* What follows is a passage from it. The passage can be found in Book IV, page 144.

> Next let us ask, if they please, out of so great a crowd of gods which the Romans worship, whom in especial, or what gods they believe to have extended and preserved that empire. Now, surely of this work, which is so excellent and so very full of the highest dignity, they dare not ascribe any part to the goddess Cloacina, or to Volupia, who has her appellation from voluptuousness; or to Libentia, who has her name from lust; or to Vaticanus who presides over the screaming of infants; or to Cunina, who rules over their cradles. But how is it possible to recount in one part of this book all the names of gods or goddesses, which they could scarcely comprise in great volumes, distributing among these divinities their peculiar offices about single things?

Pagan Rome had thousands of gods. There were gods for every little thing. They had one god for planting seed, one for germinating it, one for sprouting it, another for growing it and so on. Thousands of gods existed to grant them "benefits." Augustine says that Pagan Rome had prostituted itself to demons!

So how does this prove that he would have disapproved of the concept of "patron saints?" It is because the Roman Church has "replaced" all of these gods with patron saints. Maybe, in keeping with the concept of jabberwocky, it would be best to say that the Roman Church just renamed them as they are still performing the same "godly" functions.

The patron saints index located on the internet at http://www.catholic-forum.com/saints/indexsnt.htm lists 5,376 saints and 2,364 topics. Incidentally, Ampibolus (St. Cloak), Orestes (St. Mountain) and Veronica (Holy Handkerchief) are listed.

What are these topics? They are a list of sites or things for which one (or more) of the 5,376 saints is patron. Patron means father, protector, and benefactor. Consider that word father. Since the patron saint is supposedly helping from heaven, this word "patron" seems to imply the replacement of God in some respects. Jesus said:

> And call no man your father on the earth: for one is your Father, even he who is in heaven (Matthew 23:9 ASV).

This list of saints mated to patron duties in protecting the topics is suspiciously close to Pagan Rome's gods that Augustine wrote about. In fact, throughout the Roman Church's history, they blended the existing pagan religions with their religion in order to be politically correct. The blending was successful, they did not have to "bear the cross" and they became pagan. None of the sacraments are based upon the Word of God, and the whole issue of Mary and the saints is fiction. As Augustine stated, Pagan Rome had prostituted itself to demons. Well, it is obvious to me that the Roman Church has followed suit.

From Whence Came the Idea of Saints

There are two major teachings concerning saints. The first is through God, His Word (the Bible), and the second is the Roman Church. This is not to rule out some of the other pagan religions (of which is Rome also), but to concentrate on the differences between Rome and true Christianity.

Biblically, a saint is a believer, one who has been regenerated and indwelled by the Holy Spirit. The name saint is a description, both of what is happening to him/her and has happened to him/her. It means "set apart." Set apart for who or what? Set apart for serving God. What is happening? The indwelling Holy Spirit is "sanctifying" the saint, perfecting the saint. All believers are saints and should be serving God through the body of Christ, the local Church.

As taught by the Roman Church, however, a saint is a godlet. A godlet is a little god, replacing the demi-gods of pagan Rome. This is the "saint" that we will now trace in history.

From a Doctorial Thesis by Bessie Rebecca Burchett, entitled *Janus, in Roman Life and Cult,* 1912, published by George Banta & Co., Menasha, WI, 1918, I gleaned this information about the deification of mortal men. It may be found in chapter one.

- The first such deities developed from dead men, of whom some died naturally, and some were slain for the purpose of deifying them.
- Because people expected to receive benefits from the deified members of their tribe, the thought entered their minds that it might be advantageous to dispatch, occasionally, to the powerful company of spirits, a special representative from among the living, for, on account of his recent experience of their need, they expected him to make a greater effort on their behalf.
- The good-will of the intended victim they could easily gain beforehand by bestowing on him plentiful gifts and honors. Some victims actually looked forward to the trip.

Another aspect of this:

- In the groves, on the high places, a man roamed, always on the lookout carrying an unsheathed sword. He was a priest. His roaming and constant preparation for a fight was caused by the fact that someone was always willing to come and kill him, thereby becoming priest in his stead. The slain priest would become a god.
- These priests were called kings.
- These kings were magicians who "controlled" the weather by magic.
- The power they possessed raised their status in the eyes of their subjects, to that of a god.
- They were surrounded by gifts, privilege and taboos.
- When the crops failed, or the herds failed to increase they were slain, sacrificed, so that they could personally go to the spirits on high and plead the tribe's case.

This is the origin of the demi-gods of Rome. Jesus stated in the Bible that you can know them by their fruit. If that is the case, and it is, the fruit of the Roman Church in producing patron saints is clear. They are the same demi-gods of ancient Rome and had their origination in the previously mentioned beliefs and practices.

Notice their "magical" powers. The Roman saints, it is claimed, had the power to work miracles (magic) prior to death. In fact they had to have worked miracles or they would not have been sainted. It is claimed that they continue to work miracles plus intercede with Christ on behalf of the "faithful."

Did you notice the concept of receiving "benefits" from these gods? I have commented on this before about how all of the Roman Church ritual, prayers to Mary and the godlets (saints) are for "benefits." They say nothing about the service to the Church as is explained in Scripture, they just seek benefits. The connection of the Roman Church to such pagan history is clear. There is no connection to Christianity.

Did You Know?

Did you know that there are many rituals in the Roman Church that originated in other Pagan religions?

For instance, holy water and holy oil were a big issue in the early religion of the Chaldeans, Assyrians, and Babylonians. Then consider the guardian statues and images for repelling evil spirits. The concept of the "parish," acts of merit, female goddesses, patron saints, purgatory, pilgrimages to kiss and touch sacred objects, temples and mosques built for "saints," prayers for the dead, praying before images, confession of sins and kissing a string of beads all proceeded the Roman Church's usage of such rights.

Who pursued these things? The Chaldeans, Babylonians, Assyrians, Incas, Mayans, Egyptians and Greeks embraced one or more of these rituals.

Ceremonies similar to infant baptism, confirmation, and extreme unction were practiced by the Mayan and Inca Indians. How did the Roman Church get these from them? Simple, they did not originate this but brought it with them from the Old World when they migrated to the new. For example, there are great similarities between the Egyptian culture and that of the Mayans.

All people in the world come from just three families. They are the families of Noah. They started repopulating the earth right after the Noahic flood. The Ark landed on a mountain in Mesopotamia and all of the earth's population emigrated from this area. They carried many common customs with them. I believe that some of these rituals were also practiced within the Mediterranean civilization and Rome picked them up there.

> "Then he brought me to the door of the gate of Jehovah' house which was toward the north: and behold, there sat the women weeping for Tammuz" (Ezekiel 8:14).

The above verse refers to this practice: Ishtar, identified with the Goddess Dawkina, was the wife of Ea (one of the chief gods of the pantheon). Dawkina and Ishtar are one and the same. Ishtar (Dawkina) bore Ea a son, named Tammuz. Later Ishtar fell passionately in love with Tammuz. Tammuz was then brutally killed by a demon and Ishtar went into mourning.

On page 306 of this book we showed that the Romans teach that God loved Mary more than any other woman. It appeared that she was either espoused to the Father, the Spirit, or the Son. The pagan tradition is that the goddess fell in love with the son. This tradition is true also in Egypt, Assyria, Phoenicia, Greece, old Rome, and Canaan. New Rome merely assimilated this practice.

The New Advent, a Roman Church Online Encyclopedia, criticizes the idea that Rome adopted rituals from paganism similar to the Buddhists. It states that Catholic missionaries of the 19th century were amazed at the similarity of the Buddhist religion and their rituals. *The New Advent* claims that these rituals were adopted by the Buddhists from the Nestorian Church in the 7th Century. Nice story, but not possible. Some of these rituals were not adopted by the Catholics until later than this. The rosary, for example, was adopted by the Roman Church much later. There are enough similar rituals for you to believe that these rituals were copied by the Roman Church from the ancients.

All of this is man-made. Indeed, this is the definition of paganism. Paganism is man-made religion. This describes, precisely, the religion promoted by the Roman Church.

The Hot Spot: Purgatory

How would one describe purgatory? Here is a supposedly true description from a Roman Church authority Robert Cardinal Bellarmine (1542-1621).

> A man, named Drithelm, during a visit to the spirit world, was led on his journey by an angel in shining raimant, and proceeded, in the company of his guide, toward the rising of the sun. The travelers, at length, arrived in a valley of vast dimensions. This region, to the left, was covered with roasting furnaces, and, to the right, with icy cold, hail and snow.
>
> The whole valley was filled with human souls, which a tempest seemed to toss in all directions. The unhappy spirits, unable in the one part to bear the violent heat, leaped into the shivering cold, which again drove them into the scorching flames which cannot be extinguished.
>
> A numberless multitude of deformed souls were in this manner, whirled about and tormented without intermission in the extremes of alternate heat and cold. This, according to the angelic conductor who piloted Drithelm, is the place of chastisement for such as defer confession and amendment till the hour of death. All these, however, will, at the last day, be admitted to heaven: while many, through alms, vigils, prayers, and especially the mass, will be liberated even before the general judgment (*History of Romanism,* John Dowling D.D., page 361).

This is a silly story, but how would you better describe purgatory? No one has ever been there to tell about it, nor will anyone ever be. It is non-existent. This is meta-physics in action. It is on par with the work of Merlin the Magician or the Shamans of the Tartars/Mongols.

Purgatory, ostensibly, is a place for cleaning the "faithful" of residual sin. It is "self atonement." For the Roman Church, Christ's atonement was not adequate. Man has to pay for his own sins! Self-sanctification is what purgatory is for.

Doesn't one have to wonder how alms, vigils, prayers, and the mass would do anything for these poor deformed souls? Really, if they are there, in purgatory, to get their residual sin cleansed, how do alms, vigils, prayers, and the mass clean them up faster than the burning and freezing cited above?

Understand it is not the deformed souls that will be performing these acts of alms giving, vigils, prayers, and the mass. It will be their survivors still alive on Earth. It seems to me that the Roman Church is here prostituting God. They are saying that alms, vigils, prayers, and the mass, somehow placate God. It is similar to the Moslems, who seem to turn their god into a pimp, by teaching that a martyr will be supplied with seventy virgins when he gets to heaven. This is pure silliness.

Just what do you suppose God meant when He spoke to us and said:

> ... which is a figure for the time present; according to which are offered both gifts and sacrifices that cannot, as touching the conscience, make the worshipper perfect (Hebrews 9:9 ASV).

A History of the Concept of Purgatory

The **legitimacy of Purgatory** was uncertain at the time of the Council of Trent, although, they decided to include it in their Catechism anyway. Why do I say that it was uncertain? Thomas Cajetan (1469-1534) was the Italian Cardinal best known for his opposition to the teachings of Martin Luther and the Protestant Reformation while he was the Pope's Legate in Wittenberg, Germany.

> "If we could have any certainty of the origin of indulgences," **says Cardinal Cajetan,** "it would help us much in the disquisition of the truth of Purgatory: but we have not by writing any authority either of the Holy Scriptures, of the ancient doctors, Greek or Latin, which afford us the least knowledge thereof." (*The History of Romanism*, John Dowling D.D., Edward Walker, New York, 1853, Page 357).
>
> The truth is that Romish indulgences, such as were granted in the days of Boniface VIII, and in the time of the crusades, were dependent for all their supposed importance upon the fiction of Purgatory. It was the pretended power of the popes to remit hundreds or thousands of years of the tortures of purgatory, or, as in the case of a person who should die immediately after receiving plenary indulgence, to send that soul immediately to heaven." (ibid, page 357).

What is the history of purgatory? Augustine seems to have originated some thinking along this line. At one point in his writings, he acknowledges only two destinies for eternal habitation: heaven and hell. He claims that he could never really understand the truth because at one point it is mentioned that some will have been saved by the fire mentioned in 1 Corinthians 3:13-15:

> Each man's work shall be made manifest: for the day shall declare it, because it is revealed in fire; and the fire itself shall prove each man's work of what sort it is. If any man's work shall abide which he built thereon, he shall receive a reward. If any man's work shall be burned, he shall suffer loss: but he, himself shall be saved; yet so as through fire.

The picture here is similar to a person escaping a burning house and leaving behind all his possessions. The fire is applied to his works not to his person. It is an admonition to serve

Christ in the church. We are to serve Him according to Christ's directives from God's "owner's manual," the Bible, and not "do our own thing." If we do our own thing, we will suffer loss of reward at the rewards judgment for believers.

> Now he that planteth and he that watereth are one: but each shall receive his own reward according to his own labor —If any man's work shall abide which he built thereon, he shall receive a reward (1 Corinthians 3: 8, 14 ASV).

Augustine never arrived at a conclusion. Since this is so, one cannot claim that purgatory was an issue of faith at the end of the fifth century of Christianity.

Pope Gregory, "The Great," in the sixth century also wrote with indecision about this intermediate state between earth and heaven. But he did come to the point of teaching "the belief of a purgatorial fire, prior to the general judgment, is for trivial offences."

> Several authors have attributed to Gregory the discovery of purgatory, or rather the creator of purgatory. "Many things," says he [Gregory], "have in these last times become clear, which were formerly concealed" (*History of Romanism*, J.J. Dowling, pages 359 -360).

Pope Gregory "The Great" has done no more than claim to have added to God's Word. I have cited these verses before, but they bear repeating:

> I testify unto every man that heareth the words of the prophecy of this book, if any man shall add unto them, God shall add unto him the plagues which are written in this book: and if any man shall take away from the words of the book of this prophecy, God shall take away his part from the tree of life, and out of the holy city, which are written in this book (Revelation 22:18-19 ASV).
>
> Ye shall not add unto the word which I command you, neither shall ye diminish from it, that ye may keep the commandments of Jehovah your God which I command you (Deuteronomy 4:2 ASV).

God's written revelation of His will was complete at the end of Revelations 22. It is clear that Gregory is guilty of adding to God's Word. God has not appeared to man in visions, or dreams and has not caused man to write more Scripture since Revelation 22. This being true, Gregory the Great is in a great deal of trouble today. It is trouble that will stick to him like burning sulphur throughout eternity.

Understand what purgatory is *supposed* to be. It is posthumous atonement. In purgatory you atone for your own sin. It is the total negation of the work of atonement that Christ accomplished for mankind on the cross. It is paying for your sins yourself and saving yourself. It is the rejection of Christ! Some of the ancients understood this.

> The council of Aix la Chapelle, in 836, decided in direct opposition to posthumous satisfaction, or pardon. This synod mentions three ways of punishment for men's sins. Of these, two are in this life and one after death. "Sins," said this assembly, "are, in this world, punished by the repentance or compunction of the transgressor, and by the correction or chastisement of God. The third, after death, is tremendous and awful, when the Judge will say; depart from me, ye accursed, into everlasting fire, prepared for the devil and his angels" (ibid, page 360).

The fathers of this council knew nothing of purgatory and it was a council of the Roman Church!

We next hear of purgatory in 998. A fellow by name of Odilo opened an "extensive mart of prayers and masses for the use of souls detained in purgatory" (*History of Romanism,* J.J. Dowling, p 360). This was a "retail" operation. From this point on, Purgatory began to be the driving force for the sale of indulgences.

The apex of this selling indulgences scam was brought about by Johann Tetzel in Germany, by selling indulgences for Pope Leo X, who was raising money for building St. Peter's in Rome. Tetzel once boasted that he, with his indulgences, had saved more people than the Apostle Peter. "If a person ravished the Mother of God, I can sell him an indulgence that will assure him heaven" he boasted. It was Tetzel's activity that compelled Luther into his protest, joining Zwingle of Zurich in starting the Reformation.

A side note here. Do you recall Cardinal Cajetan's uncertainty as to the legitimacy of Purgatory? Cajetan was dispatched by the Pope to Wittenberg, Germany, to oppose Luther. Later,

Cajatan named Tetzel "Inquisitor General" to Poland. Inquisitor General means that Tetzel was in charge of the Inquisition in Poland where so-called heretics were persecuted.

But back to Purgatory, now up to the time of the Council of Trent. Remember Purgatory is, according to no less than Cardinal Cajetan, not a biblical teaching.

Cardinal Bellarmine, though, a few years later, tried to establish a biblical connection citing Second Maccabees 12:43-46. It is an interesting passage for him to have cited as it proves that either Maccabees is right and a large part of the New Testament is wrong and should be ripped out of our Bibles, or that the Jewish canon of Old Testament Scripture is correct and the Apocryphal books such as the Maccabees should be discarded.

Why do I hold this position? It is because Second Maccabees teaches heretical error. Let's look at the passage in question. The story is about a Jewish general, Juda, and some casualties after a battle. The fallen were prepared for burial, and upon them were found "amulets" of Jamnia. Amulets were like the **Scapular (a Roman Church good luck charm worn around the neck.)** They were worn to protect the wearer or to provide him/her with good fortune, or other benefits. They were the product of a heathen temple at Jamnia, a city of the Philistines. These dead soldiers had given themselves over to worshiping false gods and had rejected the living God of all.

> He took up a collection among all his soldiers, amounting to two thousand silver drachmas, which he sent to Jerusalem to provide for an expiatory sacrifice. In doing this he acted in a very excellent and noble way, inasmuch as he had the resurrection of the dead in view. For if he were not expecting the fallen to rise again, it would have been useless and foolish to pray for them in death. But if he did this with a view to the splendid reward that awaits those who had gone to rest in godliness, it was a holy and pious thought. He made atonement for the dead that they might be freed from this sin (Second Maccabees 12:43-46, *Catholic Study Bible*).

This is a rather confusing story, in that the dead soldiers were not living godly lives. They were worshipping false gods and were in rebellion against the living God. They had **not** gone to rest in godliness! Yet, Juda raises money for an atoning sacrifice at Jerusalem to free the deceased from this sin and considers them "godly."

The sacrifices at the Temple in Jerusalem were not intended for "freeing" individuals from sin and eternal punishment. They could "atone" for the sins of the people, keeping Israel square with God for the continued existence of Israel, but to provide atonement for the individual on the day of resurrection, the Temple Sacrifices **could not** do.

Consider Hebrews 10:4 (ASV)

> For it is impossible that the blood of bulls and goats should take away sins.

Their purpose was to foreshadow the sacrifice that Christ was to make.

> For the law having a shadow of the good things to come, not the very image of the thing (Hebrews 10:1 ASV).

The Mosiac Law is what is referred to here. However all such sacrifices result in the same thing. They are but a shadow of the good things to come. One of those good things was Christ and His High Priesthood. Faith in His **one** sacrifice is what begins the "process" of **salvation, justification,** and **sanctification,** which a person goes through in preparation for that great "gettin' up morning," the day of the resurrection of believers, who will then be glorified. Juda's purchased sacrifice did nothing for those unbelieving soldiers that died in battle. God does not sell faith or salvation; they are free!

Now then, which portion of the Bible do you feel more comfortable in removing: The false Deutero-Canonical (Apocryphal) books? or certain books of the New Testament such as Hebrews? Which ones should we remove? Everybody recognizes Hebrews as a legitimate book inspired of God. Only the Roman Church recognizes the Apocryphal books and these only since Trent. Books, such as Second Maccabbees were not part of the agreed canon of Scripture for the Roman Church prior to the Council of Trent. As you see, the doctrine of praying for the dead, and purgatory, as based upon this passage, is false.

Another verse quoted in support of Purgatory is 1 Peter 1:7. It, along with the 1 Corinthians and 2 Maccabees verses previously discussed is cited in *Catechism of the Catholic Church*, published by Doubleday in 1995.

> Wherein ye greatly rejoice, though now for a little while, if need be, ye have been put to grief in manifold trials, that the proof of your faith, being more precious than gold that perisheth though it is proved by fire, may be found unto praise and glory and honor at the revelation of Jesus Christ: whom not having seen ye love; on whom, though now ye see him not, yet believing, ye rejoice greatly with joy unspeakable and full of glory: receiving the end of your faith, even the salvation of your souls (1 Peter 1:6-9 ASV).

The trials discussed here are on this side of the grave, not in some nefarious chamber somewhere that is called Purgatory. The "proved by fire" reference is to the purification of the gold, not the believer. The verses preceding this shed some light on the subject.

> Blessed be the God and Father of our Lord Jesus Christ, who according to his great mercy begat us again unto a living hope by the resurrection of Jesus Christ from the dead, unto an inheritance incorruptible, and undefiled, and that fadeth not away, reserved in heaven for you, who by the power of God are guarded through faith unto a salvation ready to be revealed in the last time (1 Peter 1:3-5 ASV).

Note these things in 1 Peter 1:3-5:
- It refers to those "begat again."
- And therefore have a "living hope" – not dread or fear.
- This hope is by the resurrection of Christ from the dead.
- It is an inheritance incorruptible and undefiled,
  Undefiled: those "begat again are undefiled," need no more purification after death, because their inheritance is undefiled.
- An inheritance that will not fade away.
- Reserved not in purgatory but in heaven for those guarded by God through faith unto this salvation.

Paul says that when the believer dies, he is absent from the body and present with the Lord.

> Being therefore always of good courage, and knowing that, whilst we are at home in the body, we are absent from the Lord (for we walk by faith, not by sight); we are of good courage, I say, and are willing rather to be absent from the body, and to be at home with the Lord (1 Corinthians 5:6-8 ASV).

This is a wonderful passage at destroying the evil concept of purgatory. The source of the teachings of purgatory is not God! It is from that other being. Look at what the passage says. Either we are in the body or we are present (at home means in heaven) with the Lord.

The Credibility of The Creeds

At Trent, the "Apostles Creed" was discussed and made a part of the Roman Church catechism. The part that lends itself to the teachings about purgatory is the phrase, "He descended into hell." At Trent, they agreed:

> We profess that, immediately after the death of Christ, his soul descended into hell, and dwelt there whilst his body remained in the grave.

The Apostle's Creed states that Jesus was buried and descended into Hell. This is an outright falsehood. He did not descend into Hell. Remember what He said to the thief on the cross?

> And one of the malefactors that were hanged railed on him, saying, Art not thou the Christ? save thyself and us. But the other answered, and rebuking him said, Dost thou not even fear God, seeing thou art in the same condemnation? And we indeed justly; for we receive the due reward of our deeds: but this man hath done nothing amiss. And he said, Jesus, remember me when thou comest in thy kingdom. And he said unto him, Verily I say unto thee, today shalt thou be with me in Paradise (Luke 23:39-43 ASV).

It seems like the concept of Christ in Hell taught in the Apostle's Creed may have been the seed for the idea of purgatory. The apostles never saw the creed; if they did they would have rejected at least that portion of it.

One final point, Hell, does not necessarily mean Hell. It is translated from a variety of words. Hades, for example simply means the grave. Christ's body did descend into the grave, but His spirit, like that of the repented thief on the cross, was with God the Father in Heaven at the moment of His death. However the Roman Church clearly believes He was in Hell those three days, in spite of what Scripture says.

You Can Be Sure of Your Salvation

ESCAPE FROM PAGANISM

You can be sure of your salvation. You can be absolutely sure! How?

Look into the mirror of your heart. Do you see a sinner staring back at you? You should, as the Bible says that all have sinned and fall short of the glory of God. Further, it states that there are none righteous, no, not one, and that the wages of sin is death. But Christ died for the ungodly! He paid the penalty for your sin. If you believe in Him you will be saved, "begat again" as it says in 1 Peter, "born again" as says John. "All who call upon the name of the Lord will be saved" as says Paul in Romans 10. Read below what the Prophet Isaiah said:

> Ho, every one that thirsteth, come ye to the waters, and he that hath no money; come ye, buy, and eat; yea, come, buy wine and milk without money and without price. Wherefore do ye spend money for that which is not bread? and your labor for that which satisfieth not? hearken diligently unto me, and eat ye that which is good, and let your soul delight itself in fatness. Incline your ear, and come unto me; hear, and your soul shall live.
>
> Seek ye Jehovah while he may be found; call ye upon him while he is near: let the wicked forsake his way, and the unrighteous man his thoughts; and let him return unto Jehovah, and he will have mercy upon him; and to our God, for he will abundantly pardon. For my thoughts are not your thoughts, neither are your ways my ways, saith Jehovah. For as the heavens are higher than the earth, so are my ways higher than your ways, and my thoughts than your thoughts. For as the rain cometh down and the snow from heaven, and returneth not thither, but watereth the earth, and maketh it bring forth and bud, and giveth seed to the sower and bread to the eater; so shall my word be that goeth forth out of my mouth: it shall not return unto me void, but it shall accomplish that which I please, and it shall prosper in the thing whereto I sent it (Excerpts from Isaiah 55 ASV).

Seek the Lord, repent, and be pardoned - saved! You can do this right where you are and be assured of heaven when you are called home. **Assured** - nothing left to chance - assured of your eternal salvation.

A Parade

You are standing in a crowd at the side of a road. The road leads to a great stone temple. There is a holy parade in progress. There are quite a number of priests and acolytes marching down the street. They are all decked out in their finest costumes.

Many of the priests and acolytes, who walk in groups of four, are carrying litters upon which a small child is seated. Each child is dressed in a pretty robe, and has garlands in its hair. There are maybe fifty or so of these. From the looks of the children, though, they are all terrified. Tears are flowing down their faces. They appear to be screaming "Mommy, Mommy," but you cannot hear them because the drums, cymbals, bells, and chanting are making so much noise. All this noise is by design, to keep the people from being guilt-ridden by the screams and cries of these babies.

What is this parade for? Where are they taking the children? It is a holy day to the gods. So, what about the children?

The children are being taken to the Temple to be sacrificed—that means killed, slaughtered! They are to be killed to placate the gods. One by one, they will be laid on top of the altar with two priests each holding a leg, and two priests each holding an arm; the child will be held firmly in place. Another priest with a long obsidian knife, plunges his instrument into the breast of the helpless child, ripping a big hole and then carving out the heart. He holds it high, dripping the life blood of the child, as an offering to the gods. What an honor for these children, right?

Yes, this is a horrible story. This one took place frequently in Mexico and the crime was committed by the Aztecs. The priests, in this case, would purchase the children from poor people.

Human Sacrifice Was Common

It is also true that pagan Rome, Greece, Asia, Assyria, Canaan, Babylon and others (worldwide) practiced human sacrifices of some sort. In Rome, human sacrifice was still being practiced after the crucifixion of Christ.

Even the Jews were enticed into offering their first born to Molech, a brass statue with a human form for a body, and the head of a bull for a head. Hollow inside, a fire was built and Molech became a furnace. The first-born of the family making the sacrifice would either be placed on the white hot arms of the idol or dropped into a pit of coals in front of it. Again, drums, symbols, and horns would drown the screams and cries of the burning child.

> And thou shalt not give any of thy seed to make them pass through the fire to Molech; neither shalt thou profane the name of thy God: I am Jehovah (Leviticus 18:21 ASV).

> Moreover, thou shalt say to the children of Israel, Whosoever he be of the children of Israel, or of the strangers that sojourn in Israel, that giveth of his seed unto Molech; he shall surely be put to death: the people of the land shall stone him with stones. I also will set my face against that man, and will cut him off from among his people; because he hath given of his seed unto Molech, to defile my sanctuary, and to profane my holy name. And if the people at the land do at all hide their eyes from that man, when he giveth of his seed unto Molech, and put him not to death; then I will set my face against that man, and against his family, and will cut him off, and all that play the harlot after him, to play the harlot with Molech, from among their people (Leviticus 20:2-5 ASV).

> And they built the high places of Baal, which are in the valley of the son of Hinnom, to cause their sons and their daughters to pass through the fire unto Molech; which I commanded them not, neither came it into my mind, that they should do this abomination, to cause Judah to sin (Jeremiah 32:35 ASV).

"Christianity" Legitimized By Emperor Constantine

Escape From Paganism

Before "Christianity" was legitimized in the Roman Empire by Constantine, sacrifice of Christians was common. They were fed to wild beasts, used as torches for "night games," burned at the stake, and beheaded. These were just the common means of sacrifice.

I say before "Christianity" was legitimized by Constantine with just a little sarcasm. Constantine's imperious action sped the perversion of true Christianity. He did not legitimize it. From his "so called" conversion, many pagan elements began to filter into the church and soon the visible, legal church was no longer the body of Christ, but subject to the new Emperor of Rome, the Pope of the Church of Rome.

Under the auspices of the Roman Church, human sacrifice continued until at least 1821, though, as late as the 1850s people were still being imprisoned under sentences of death in the Roman Church principalities such as Bologna, Italy. This human sacrifice was called the "Inquisition." Was the inquisition a sacrifice to the gods? Well, judge for yourself. Consider this term: "Auto de fe."

> The phrase **auto de fe** refers to the ritual of public penance of condemned apostates that took place when the Spanish Inquisition or the Portuguese Inquisition had decided their punishment (that is, after the trial). Auto de fé in medieval Spanish means "act of faith."
>
> The auto de fe involved: a Catholic Mass; prayer; a public procession of those found guilty; and a reading of their sentences (Peters 1988: 93-94). They took place in public squares or esplanades and lasted several hours: ecclesiastical and civil authorities attended. Artistic representations of the auto de fe usually depict torture and the burning at the stake– an auto de fe, which was in essence a religious act.
>
> In chapter VI of satire, *Candide*, an Auto-de-fe is held in the Portuguese capital after the disastrous 1755 Lisbon earthquake, because the citizens are convinced that the earthquake was a punishment from God. Dr. Pangloss is captured for making a speech, and hanged, after which another tremendous earthquake occurs. The

Leonard Bernstein operetta of *Candide*, turns this into a satirical song called "Auto-de-fe," where the citizens of Lisbon cheerfully sing "What a day, what a day for an auto-de-fe" as they witness the hanging of Jews and heretics. (www. wikipedia.org/wiki/Auto_de_fe).

The "Auto de fe" was the torture phase of a condemned heretics "passion." Who was considered a "heretic?" They were professing Christians who were not members of the Roman Church and the Jews. Here are some "invigorating" examples of an "Auto de fe" or "act of faith."

> Thumbscrews, toescrews and knee-splitters also were used to crack, pop or break the joints or splinter the bones of a suspect. Tongues were pierced, cut or rooted out and eyes extinguished by gouging, plucking, bursting or burning. Ears, noses, hands and feet were sawn, cut or hacked off; toes and fingers were amputated – sometimes joint by joint over several days.

These are just a few of the many descriptions of the "acts of faith" a condemned heretic might be subject to. Here is a final one, it is a quote from Fr. Marianus de Luca.

> Let the women gaze on this horrible piece of ingenuity, the spider! It is a cluster of steel hooks pointed like needles. It is designed to be spread over the breast of the woman; the hand of the torturer grasps the central ring, drawing the points together, and then the flesh is torn away (*Thumbscrew and Rack* by Geo E. Macdonald).

All of these examples and **many** others can be read in *666, the antichrist's almanac, 2000 Online Edition*. The address is www.antichrist.com.

Keep in mind that the *Auto de fe* was a religious offering of the Roman Church to their god as a propitiation for either the general sins of the public (such as after an earthquake), or to propitiate the "sin" of allowing heretics to exist at all and thereby gain "benefits" from God in the form of no more disaster.

Yet Another Parade

Let's examine another parade, one that is much worse than the previously portrayed parade in Mexico. It is a parade that has gone on for maybe 1,700 years and continues today. The Roman Church, by its false teaching, has been leading men, women, and children down the road to destruction all those years. The result, as we shall see, is horrible beyond words.

As a side note, though, there is no reason to exclude the false teaching of any other church for that matter. Any church that teaches that salvation is transmitted to a person by a sacrament, or that by good works of any sort, a person can be saved, is as guilty of false teaching as is the Roman Church.

Have you ever seen the Champs-Élysées in Paris? It is a **broad** avenue, and the scenery is very beautiful. Some have termed it the most beautiful avenue in the world. Lovers walk up and down this avenue, telling each other – well who knows, is there a limit under the circumstances? It is a great place just for a stroll. Such beauty and serenity can be deceptive.

> Enter ye in by the narrow gate: for wide is the gate, and **broad** is the way, that leadeth to destruction, and many are they that enter in thereby. For narrow is the gate, and straitened the way, that leadeth unto life, and few are they that find it (Matthew 7:13-14 ASV).

These are Jesus' words, describing the way to destruction and unto life. The priests of the Roman Church, with its sacraments, good works, Mary, the saints and their relics, have been marching people, adults and children, down the broad way for centuries. Why do I say broad? Let's review their multi-faceted concept of how salvation is "earned" by those in their parade.

BAPTISMAL REGENERATION

According to their teaching, the grace of their god is transmitted to the "victim" through baptism. This "grace" remits original sin. If a person dies prior to committing a sin, then that person is saved.

PENANCE/CONFESSION

Any sin committed after baptism must be confessed and penance (some work by the penitent) must be performed to regain salvation. A distinction is made by the Roman Church between venial sin and mortal sin. It is my understanding that they are concerned here about mortal sin. Venial sin is taken care of in another way. The grace of their god reaches through this ritual/work and remits the sins confessed.

EUCHARIST/MASS

This is where the Roman Church kills Christ over and over again. The mass is a sacrifice. It is a sacrifice of Christ. His one sacrifice on the cross is not accepted as adequate by the Roman Church. The mass is taken by the communicant for remittance of his/her personal sin, plus the mass can be taken (how about performed) for the dead who are in purgatory.

EXTREME UNCTION

This is commonly known as the last rights. The claim is that the dying person's sin can be remitted through this ritual. Again, it is claimed that the grace of their god reaches the dying person through this sacrament.

PURGATORY

This is the place where the Roman Church claims that a person atones for his/her own sin. It is a place of "sensible" purification. In other words, the person undergoing the cleansing will feel the pain. According to some Roman Church teaching it can take many thousands of years to accomplish. For example, in the book, *Vatican Council II,* on page 412, this statement is made:

> This sacred council (Vatican II) accepts loyally the venerable faith of our ancestors in the living communion which exists between us and our brothers who are in the glory of heaven or who are yet being purified after their death; and it proposes again the decrees of the

Second Council of Nicea, of the Council of Florence, and of the Council of Trent.

Second Nicea was about 1,200 years ago. Those that attended were Roman Church leaders. What Vatican II is saying is that there is a good chance that purgatory holds sinful church leaders from these and other councils. Who can tell how many of the regular members, are being held in purgatory? The answer, of course, is none, as purgatory does not exist!

GODDESS MARY AND ALL THE LITTLE GODLETS

We have seen how the Roman Church has elevated Mary and the saints to the position of goddess and "little gods." Mary now assumes the same position in the Roman Church that Diana/Minerva/Venus/Astarte/Kali did and does for the pagan religions. Why the forward slashes rather than commas? They all signify the same woman.

The saints assume the same position as the "duty" gods or demi-gods did and do for the pagans. The one, true, living God was and is not adequate for the Roman Church.

THE PRIESTS

The Roman Church claims to have the keys to heaven and to have the power to admit or exclude someone from heaven. The power includes, they believe, the power to absolve a person from sin. Their priest has the power and their god can say nothing against their decision, as he delegated that authority to them. We have seen it claimed that the priest, in this regard is more powerful than their god.

The Roman Church is honest in one thing: they never assure you of your salvation. With their system of sacraments and other invented devices, it would be unprofitable to them to have a system of assurance.

The Roman Church has led this parade of children and adults down the wide path to destruction. The difference between the parade of children to be sacrificed at the Aztec Temple and the people in the Roman Church is that those in the Roman Church parade are blissful, thinking that their church is protecting them from hell, when it is not. They are taught that they have no personal concern as the church has the keys and makes all the spiritual decisions. The "faithful" really have no responsibility except to do as the church instructs them. This is false teaching! Each person has the individual responsibility to come to know and to decide for Christ.

How are they headed for destruction? They are headed for the judgment seat of Christ and the Lake of Fire.

> And I saw a great white throne, and him that sat upon it, from whose face the earth and the heaven fled away; and there was found no place for them. And I saw the dead, the great and the small, standing before the throne; and books were opened: and another book was opened, which is the book of life: and the dead were judged out of the things which were written in the books, according to their works. And the sea gave up the dead that were in it; and death and Hades gave up the dead that were in them: and they were judged every man according to their works. And death and Hades were cast into the lake of fire. This is the second death, even the lake of fire. And if any was not found written in the book of life, he was cast into the lake of fire (Revelation 20: 21 ASV).

The Book of Revelation, the last book in the Bible, describes God's final judgments upon this earth and its rebellious inhabitants. The contents of Revelation were revealed to the Apostle John who was exiled to the Island of Patmos off the coast of Turkey.

The Great White Throne is the judgment seat of the Lord Jesus Christ. The time is at the close of His thousand-year-reign from the Throne of David at Jerusalem. The Devil has already been cast into the Lake of Fire, thereby beginning his eternal punishment.

Many others will also begin their eternal punishment. They are those whose names are not found written in the Book of Life. All of these will suffer the "second death." Have you ever wondered about yourself? What is your eternal destiny? Will you be with the Devil, suffering constantly the agony of the second death?

The Great White Throne Judgment

Again, you are in a large crowd. You can see, way up in front, a Great White Throne. The man who sits in the throne is the Lord Jesus Christ. It is judgment day. Person after person approaches the Throne, bows, and then kneels before Him with outstretched arms. After just few words, angels come and carry the person from in front of the throne to a dark area over on the horizon. Each time a shudder radiates through the crowd.

... that person is headed for "outer darkness" some whisper (see Matthew 22:13 ASV).

... to the Lake of Fire say others (see Revelation 20:10-15 ASV).

It makes little difference what they say, as both are the same place and it is a place where no one wishes to spend eternity.

Slowly you advance towards the Throne. As you get closer you see a second crowd of people. They are all praising God and the Lamb, Jesus Christ. For them it appears to be a day of victory.

Wait, who is that whom you are looking at? It is your Aunt Sophia. She is in that happy crowd. She is the one that always made you angry because she was constantly preaching at you about Jesus Christ and the need for you to place your faith in Him alone, regardless of what the Roman Church had to say. You remember the day that you told her in no uncertain terms that you were fed up with her preaching and that you never wanted to see her again.

There is another face you recognize; it is your son Michael. He left the Roman Church and was banished by the family for doing the same thing that Aunt Sophia did. He is in that happy crowd also. You look around with some satisfaction, though, as most of your family, generations of grandparents, your children and several generations of grandchildren that came along after your death, are right there with you–all headed for the Throne.

Finally you are number two from being able to talk to the Lord. The man in front of you has just bowed and fallen to his knees. The Lord asks him, "Why should I let you into my heaven?"

The man holds out his hands and says, "Lord, I was baptized, confirmed, went regularly to confession and did penance, took mass and participated in the eucharist frequently, had the last rights, paid money for masses for the dead, had my sins absolved by the Bishop, said the rosary daily, prayed to Mary and the saints to intercede on my behalf with you, venerated the images, and the relics of the saints. Lord I have worked hard to do all these things faithfully so that I could spend eternity in heaven."

Wow, you think, *he said all the things I am going to say.* Then you go into shock. The Lord tells the man, "Depart from me I never knew you!" The angels come and haul him away (see Matthew 7:23 & 25:41).

Now it is your turn. It suddenly hits you. You are headed for the second death, eternal fire, and so are all of your family members.

"Why, oh why," you say, "did I not listen to Aunt Sophia and my son, Michael?"

The Judgment

Revelation 21:25 references those whose names are not written in the Book of Life, and will therefore be sent to the Lake of Fire. What kind of people will not be in the Book of Life and therefore judged according to their works?

> But for the fearful, and **unbelieving**, and abominable, and murderers, and fornicators, and sorcerers, and **idolaters**, and all liars, their part shall be in the lake that burneth with fire and brimstone; which is the second death (Revelation 21:8).

Notice the inclusion of **unbelievers** and **idolaters**. Think of the images or icons in the Roman Church that are venerated. This is idolatry! Do you remember our discussion about how you can be born again? John 3:16 says that salvation is through belief upon the Lord Jesus Christ. **At least sixteen times** in the Book of John, we are called upon to believe in Christ, **sixteen times!**

Jesus said:

> Let the evildoer still do evil, and the filthy still be filthy, and the righteous still do right, and the holy still be holy (Revelation 22:11).

Could it be said that you are one who "does right and is holy?" What do you think? Years ago, I was somewhat shocked to find out what God's assessment of me was. More shocking is that His assessment of me was not unique to me, but applies to all mankind, even you.

Here is what Jesus says:

> Romans 3:10 – "As it is written, 'There is none righteous, not even one!'"
>
> Romans 3:12 – "All have turned aside, together they have become useless, there is none who does good, there is not even one."
>
> Romans 3:23 – "For all have sinned and come short of the glory of God!"

All! Did you notice the word **all** and **none**? That includes Mary and the little godlets, the saints. All of them and us have sinned; none of us are righteous. The reason I mention goddess Mary and the little godlets is that they supposedly earned excess merit by their works in this life and this super abundance of merit is on deposit for our use in the Roman Church's heaven. No merit exists in any treasury because neither Mary nor the godlets earned any. They were not righteous, they did no good (in and of themselves). They sinned, they came short of the glory of God (the real living God, not the fictitious god of the Roman Church). They needed the mercy and grace of God available through Christ, just as do the rest of us.

Further, this problem began early in the history of man and has been epidemic since.

> Romans 5:12 - "Through one man sin entered into the world, and death through sin; and so death passed unto all men, for that all sinned."
>
> Romans 6:23 - "The wages of sin is death."

This is really a pretty dismal assessment of us by God. None righteous, useless, none that do good, all have sinned – yes, a pretty dismal assessment, especially in light of the words of Christ in those final hours:

Let the evildoer still do evil, and the filthy still be filthy, and the righteous still do right, and the holy still be holy.

Earlier I asked you, "What kind of people will not be in the Book of Life and therefore judged according to their works?" I then quoted some verses describing those people, but as we have seen all of us are sinners and all of us would fit the description of those not in the Book of Life and sent to the Lake of Fire.

I do not know about you, but as for me, I would do anything to avoid the Second Death. It is eternity in the Lake of Fire. It is worse than being dragged up the steps of some Aztec Temple and having your heart carved out with an obsidian stone knife. It is an eternity of death. But this eternity of death is not without sensual awareness – it is an eternity of constant suffering.

But you might say, "Sinner? Who says I am a sinner? I do a pretty good job being a 'good neighbor' and am a pretty decent person! I am just not a bad person!" In response to this kind of attitude, the Apostle John, under inspiration from God, wrote these words:

> If we say that we have no sin, we deceive ourselves, and the truth is not in us (1 John 1:8).

We are not comparing "big" sinners with "little" sinners. All are guilty of sin. But if all of mankind is guilty of sin, then what else could be in store for you and for me? Is there any way to avoid this destiny? Is there any "salvation" for sinners? If so, how is it obtained and can it be guaranteed? How can we be holy and proclaimed by the Lord that we will remain ***holy***? Is there anything that we can **do**?

The purpose of this book has been to discuss and compare the Roman Church dogma to the Word of God. My goal has been to show the reader the vast difference between how the Roman Church says one may attain Heaven and how the Word of God says one may attain Heaven. We must choose the Bible as our authority, it is of God. The stakes are high, so we must make the right choice. Jesus said:

> For narrow is the gate, and straitened the way, that leadeth unto life, and few are they that find it (Matthew 7:14).

Victory In Jesus

See what is in store for us if we do "find" the way.

> And I saw a new heaven and a new earth: for the first heaven and the first earth are passed away; and the sea is no more. And I saw the holy city, new Jerusalem, coming down out of heaven from God, made ready as a bride adorned for her husband. And I heard a great voice out of the throne saying, Behold, the tabernacle of God is with men, and he shall dwell with them, and they shall be his peoples, and God himself shall be with them, and be their God: and he shall wipe away every tear from their eyes; and death shall be no more; neither shall there be mourning, nor crying, nor pain, any more: the first things are passed away. And he that sitteth on the throne said, Behold, I make all things new. And he saith, Write: for these words are faithful and true. And he said unto me, They are come to pass. I am the Alpha and the Omega, the beginning and the end. I will give unto him that is athirst of the fountain of the water of life freely. He that overcometh shall inherit these things; and I will be his God, and he shall be my son (Revelation 21:1-7).

You see here a new heaven and a new earth, a new Jerusalem, the Holy City, and the "Alpha and Omega, who is the Lord and God, Jesus Christ. You also see an existence for those who inhabit this place that is without pain, mourning, tears, death or anything bad. It is eternal life as life was meant to be – a life of joy, peace, security, vigor, and constantly replenished by the water of life. Can you be one that overcomes and inherit these things?

How do we attain to this place? It will not be by the Roman Church's sacraments, goddesses, or "godlets" (saints), their relics or the images (idols) that represent their god, goddess, and godlets. Dependence upon these things will only destine you for the Lake of Fire. Nor will indulgences or absolution by a priest, bishop, cardinal or pope get you there.

The way to the New Jerusalem is through faith in Christ, and faith in Christ alone. Let me say it again: there is nothing that can get you into the new heaven and new earth except faith in the atoning work of Christ.

Christ:
- Is the Son of God, the Son of Man, fully God and fully man.
- All things were made through Him.
- Is our Prophet.
- Is our Priest.
- Is our King.
- Is the Second Adam, a new race of mankind without a sin nature.
- Is our **one** sacrifice for our sin.
- Was crucified, dead, and buried.
- Was resurrected from the dead.
- Lives today.
- Is our Savior.
- Is the Head of **His** church of which believers are all Living Stones and members of His body,
- Will be King forever on the Throne of David.

This is the Christ that we must believe in. We must believe in Him as our Lord and as our Savior. The Book of Romans says:

> If thou shalt confess with thy mouth Jesus as Lord, and shalt believe in thy heart that God raised him from the dead, thou shalt be saved: for with the heart man believeth unto righteousness; and with the mouth confession is made unto salvation (Romans 10:9-10 ASV).

Remember the news release from the current pope, claiming that the Roman Church is the sole source of salvation. He is wrong! You cannot be saved by the dogma, liturgy, or sacraments of the Roman Church. Believe them and you will find yourself deceived into eternal destruction.

Sola Scriptura, Sola Fidae, Sola Christus was the cry of the Protestants in the 16th century. These Latin words mean only Scripture, and only faith. The only source of the truth of God as relates to salvation is the Scriptures, the Word of the Living God. The only path to salvation is faith in the Son of God, Jesus Christ. This faith results in your regeneration, the New Birth, wherein the Spirit of God takes up residence in your life.

The New Birth is permanent because you are a new you, born into the family of God, a brother/sister to Christ. You cannot be unborn. From the point of your new birth to the point that God brings you home, you are being sanctified. God, through His Word, and His discipline, will make you perfect. There is absolutely no uncertainty about this. It is God's will that it **will** happen. There is no purgatory. If God calls you home, you will be absent from the body, but instantaneously in the presence of the Lord. Think of this - it is blessed assurance!

Is this something that you want? Do you want eternal life in the presence of the Lord? You can have it, it is free to you, and the Lord Jesus paid the supreme price for it. I can remember the struggle that I went through. I finally prayed to the Lord and told Him of my struggle. I told Him that what I had been told, what I had read, I wanted, but was having trouble with believing. I had no problem with admitting my sinfulness, just trouble believing that all this was real. So I asked the Lord to help me with my unbelief, and He did. He sent the Holy Spirit into my heart and gave me a new one.

As I write this the year is 2008. It was thirty-six years ago that my eternal life began. It was thirty-six years ago that the Lord took control and began to change me. It was thirty-six years ago that I gained the Blessed Hope. What about you?

You can have the Blessed Hope. Just tell God that you know you are a sinner, that you know you deserve His punishment for your sin, that you know that the wages of sin is death. Tell Him you do not want to pay that price and wish to cast yourself on the atoning sacrifice of Christ, that you believe Christ died for you and that you want to place your faith in Him. Ask God for help in this. It is between you and Him. You do not need a priest for this. Christ is your high priest and He will intercede for you. The newness of your eternal life begins at the instant of your faith.

It is my hope that we meet in heaven as part of that victorious crowd and not the one that shuffles forward for judgment.

Appendix
Successors of Peter? Really?

This information was derived from the book *Is the Roman Church Holy?* You can obtain a copy of this book, free, by downloading it from www.archive.org. I recommend that you do. It is short, but a very revealing and interesting book.

YEAR	POPE	NOTABLE EVENTS OR CHARACTER
358	**Liberius**	Armed struggle with Felix over the Bishopric of Rome. (ITRCH pg. 36)
358	**Felix**	See above; many killed. (ITRCH pg. 36)
418	**Boniface I**	Blood was shed in the struggle for this pope to take control. Also the Bishop of Rome was not yet universal bishop, and would not be until the seventh century. (ITRCH pg. 41)
556	**Sylverus**	This pope was "the illegitimate son of celibate Pope Hormisdas," and paid a large sum of money to Emperor Theodatus for the papal throne. (ITRCH pg. 52)
606	**Boniface III**	The seat of the empire at this time was Constantinople. The Emperor Phocus had murdered the Empress and her daughter. Therefore, the Byzantine Church refused him admission. In revenge, Phocus made the Bishop of Rome the Universal Pope over all the churches. Boniface III was, therefore, the first universal pope. He was raised to that position by a murderer and not by the Holy Spirit, apostolic succession, or succession from Peter! (ITRCH pg. 53)

Abbreviation: ITRCH = *Is The Roman Church Holy?* by J. A. Henderson

ESCAPE FROM PAGANISM

YEAR	POPE	NOTABLE EVENTS OR CHARACTER
625	**Honorius**	Judged to be a heretic after his death by the General Council at Constantinople in 681. If a heretic, would not this break the chain of apostolic succession claimed by the Roman Church? (ITRCH pg. 54)
654	**Eugene**	Made pope by the Emperor to replace Martin I. Martin and Eugene were both popes at the same time. Two infallible popes at once, they did not agree with each other. How could this be? (ITRCH pg. 54)
678	**Agatho**	The first to claim papal infallibility. "All the constitutions of the Roman Church are to be received as if they had been delivered by the divine voice of St. Peter." Peter is now stated to be a god (divine voice). (ITRCH pg. 55)
742	**St. Zachary**	Conspired with Pepen to overthrow the King of the Franks, Chideric III. Zachary, on his part was willing to betray his sovereign, Constantine V, of the Eastern Roman Empire, regardless of what God says in His Word about obeying leaders. The Roman Church sainted this Pope so that he is now worshipped as a god. Yes, I know that they say "venerated" but the word "venerate" means to worship. Worship refers to what you do towards a god – even a false one such as Zachary (ITRCH pg. 58)
767	**Constantine**	He was a layman that took the papacy by force of arms. He did not go through the orders, or have hands laid on him. According to Roman Church beliefs and their canon law, the apostolic succession was broken with this pope. (ITRCH pg. 64)

Abbreviation: ITRCH = *Is The Roman Church Holy?* by J. A. Henderson

YEAR	POPE	NOTABLE EVENTS OR CHARACTER
855	**Popess Joan**	Female pope, labeled as a fable by some of the Roman Church. Labeled as true by others, such as that most Catholic of university leaders: Gerson of the University of Paris. The Dominicans also support the fact of "la papessa." (ITRCH pg. 67)
872	**John VIII**	The Bishop of Naples, Athanasius, murdered his brother the Duke of Naples, making himself, thereby, the Duke-Bishop of Naples. This pope confirmed the legitimacy of Athanasius' actions as being divinely inspired. In other words, Athanasius murdered his brother at God's command. (ITRCH pg. 69)
891	**Formosus**	Participated in the murder of Pope John VIII. He was excommunicated for this crime but still elected pope. Anyone for apostolic succession here? (ITRCH pg. 71)
901	**Stephen VII**	Strangled – probably deserved it. (ITRCH pg. 71)
904	**Leo V**	Thrown into prison after a forty day rule, by his servant Christopher, who usurped the Holy See. (ITRCH pg.73)
910	**Sergius III**	At the head of a military force, took the throne of the Roman Church. Sergius had a mistress by the name of Marozia. She had a son by Sergius named Octavian. He was made pope, by her, at the age of 18. He became John XI. Marozia, her mother Theodora, and sister Theodora, were in control of the papacy. Apostolic succession, anyone? (ITRCH pg. 73)

Abbreviation: ITRCH = *Is The Roman Church Holy?* by J. A. Henderson

ESCAPE FROM PAGANISM

YEAR	POPE	NOTABLE EVENTS OR CHARACTER
955	**John XII**	Became pope at age 19. He was extremely immoral. At the urging of the German ecclesiastics, Emperor Otho intervened, held a trial at Rome and deposed John. Otho's reign was the beginning of the Holy Roman Empire. (ITRCH pg. 73)
972	**John XIII**	Expelled from Rome but reinstated with the help of Otho. He exacted terrible reprisals and after five years in the throne, he was strangled. (ITRCH pg. 78)
973	**Benedict VI**	Strangled. (ITRCH pg. 78)
984	**Boniface VII**	Boniface strangled Benedict VI and elevated himself to pope. He was pope for one month but had to flee for his life. (ITRCH pg. 78)
984	**John XV**	Had his feet, hands and tongue cut out by Gregory V. See below. (ITRCH pg. 78)
995	**Gregory V**	Usurped the papal throne with the help of Otho, the Holy Roman Emperor. He cut off the feet, hands and tongue of John XV, and did the same to one other person. He then made them walk through the streets of Rome, mutilated and bleeding. Apostolic succession? (ITRCH pg. 79)
999	**Sylvester II**	Poisoned. (ITRCH pg. 80)
1033	**Benedict IX**	Five times pope. The first time was as a boy aged 11. Apostolic succession? (ITRCH pg. 81-83)

Abbreviation: ITRCH = *Is The Roman Church Holy?* by J. A. Henderson

YEAR	POPE	NOTABLE EVENTS OR CHARACTER
1058	**Benedict X**	Placed in the papal chair by armed force. A schism was created when the opposition named Nicholas II as pope. Infallibility? (ITRCH pg. 84)
1061	**Nicholas II**	One of two popes, each contending with each other with armed bands, allied bishops with gangs roving and killing each other. What was it that Christ told Pilate? Wasn't it "If my kingdom was of this world then would my servants fight?" These Roman Church leaders certainly were not servants of Christ. (ITRCH pg. 84)
1073	**Gregory VII**	Given name was Hildebrand. He usurped the papacy and claimed to be Lord, spiritual and temporal of the entire world. He thought the papacy was the civil authority of all as well as the spiritual authority. He was rumored to have poisoned a pope. He had a very wealthy mistress. (ITRCH pg. 85)
1130	**Honorius II**	Heretics have no rights – and "all heretics, of both sexes and of every name, we damn to perpetual infamy; we declare hostility against them; we account them accursed, and their goods confiscated." If the church is infallible does not this decree still stand? (ITRCH pg. 86)
1144	**Lucius II**	Stoned to death. (ITRCH pg. 88)
1159	**Alexander III**	Armed struggle for the Holy See against Pope Victor, many died. There was a succession of four popes opposing him. (ITRCH pg. 88)
1216	**Innocent III**	Instigated the Crusade against the Albigensis. He made this famous (infamous) statement, "We have taken the place of God upon the earth." (ITRCH pg. 96)

Abbreviation: ITRCH = *Is The Roman Church Holy?* by J. A. Henderson

YEAR	POPE	NOTABLE EVENTS OR CHARACTER
1241	**Colestine IV**	A controversial choice, died (murdered) after serving but a few days. (ITRCH pg. 98)
1248	**Innocent IV**	He established the permanent court of inquisition. If the church is infallible, does not this office still exist? (ITRCH pg. 98)
1268	**Clement IV**	Murdered. (ITRCH pg. 101)
1276	**Innocent V**	Poisoned by the Cardinals that elected him shortly after his election. (ITRCH pg. 102)
1277	**Nicholas III**	He pillaged churches and monasteries and begged for money in every court to enrich his family. Within a few years his relatives went from being poor to being the richest lords of Italy. (ITRCH pg. 105)
1285	**Martin IV**	He was called the "Lamb of God" – one of the titles of Christ. This man was professing to be Christ. Note above that Innocent III claimed to be God on earth. (ITRCH pg. 106)
1277	**Nicholas III**	Gave the Dominicans charge of the Inquisition. To do this he gave them free reign to interpret ecclesiastical laws. Heretics had no rights. (ITRCH pg. 105)
1292	**Colestine V**	Allowed himself to be hoodwinked out of the office of pope by the succeeding Pope Boniface VIII (ITRCH pg. 108)
1294	**Boniface VIII**	Placed in hell by Dante. Through "spookery," he caused Pope Colestine to resign as pope (admitting his fallibility) thereby paving the way to the papal throne for Boniface. (ITRCH pg. 108)

Abbreviation: ITRCH = *Is The Roman Church Holy?* by J. A. Henderson

YEAR	POPE	NOTABLE EVENTS OR CHARACTER
1316	**John XXII**	John speculated in human corruption and sold absolution. He was the first to add the third crown to the tiara, symbolizing the power of the popes over heaven, earth, and hell. (ITRCH pg. 114)
1334	**Benedict XII**	Remembered by the Roman Church as a heretic. Now just what happened to that "apostolic succession" routine? (ITRCH pg. 117)
1342	**Clement VI**	Had a mistress who sold church offices. Tetrarch stated about this pope, and his court, "their white hair and ample togas, concealed an impudence and lasciviousness which nothing equals." (ITRCH pg. 118)
1362	**Urban V**	Mysterious death caused either by the husband of his mistress, Joanna, Queen of Naples, or by the Cardinals who were plotting against him. (ITRCH pg. 122)
1370	**Gregory XI**	Made pope at age 18. As he needed money, he got the idea of finding and burning heretics, then seizing their property. Crusades against the Vaudois and Albigenesis were instigated. One of the Bishop/Generals ordered all the people in a particular city in southern France to be slaughtered. His orders were to kill all, including members of the Roman Church. "God will know His own," said he. (ITRCH pg. 123)
1378	**Urban VI**	In a conflict with the French over Avignon, he ordered all the French inhabitants of Rome slaughtered –all men, women, and children. He murdered several ecclesiastics who came to the Vatican to implore mercy. (ITRCH pg. 126)

Abbreviation: ITRCH = *Is The Roman Church Holy?* by J. A. Henderson

YEAR	POPE	NOTABLE EVENTS OR CHARACTER
1389	**Boniface IX**	An Italian pope opposed to the French pope at Avignon. A long schism was in progress. Throughout popery, at times there were multiple popes. How did apostolic succession work in such circumstances? (ITRCH pg. 128)
1394	**Benedict XIII**	Schism with Gregory XII. Theodoric, a Roman Church historian, stated, "These two wretches have cauterized consciences." (ITRCH pg. 129)
1409	**Alexander V**	Poisoned by Balthasar Cosa, who then made himself pope. (ITRCH pg. 131)
1410	**John XXIII**	His given name was Balthasar Cosa. He and his two brothers were Neapolitan pirates. He poisoned Alexander V and seized the throne by force. At this time there was another pope at Avignon, and still another in Spain. To end this schism was one of the purposes for which the Council of Constance (the council that burned Jon Hus) was called. The council deposed him and convicted him of murder and other crimes. John fled to Florence and died there. (ITRCH pg. 132)
1417	**Martin V**	All treaties or agreements with heretics were an insult to God and did not have to be honored. This was just a couple of years after the burning of Hus and his associate Jerome of Prague. If you will recall, their safe conduct agreement was dishonored by the Council of Constance on this basis. (ITRCH pg. 135)
1431	**Eugenious IV**	The illegitimate son of Gregory XII. (ITRCH pg. 137)
1439	**Felix V**	Drunk on election. (ITRCH pg. 138)

Abbreviation: ITRCH = *Is The Roman Church Holy?* by J. A. Henderson

YEAR	POPE	NOTABLE EVENTS OR CHARACTER
1458	**Pius II**	Claimed to be a votary of Venus and Bacchus. Votary means that he had made religious vows to these pagan gods. He was, therefore, an avowed pagan. He stated openly, that the gifts of the Holy Spirit could be sold. Also stated in an encyclical letter that "It did not matter whether a pope were moral or immoral, a saint, or a devil, that he (the pope) became the Almighty. By the mere act of exaltation of the pope, he is God Himself!" Considering the infallibility of the pope and the Roman Church, would this not still be the belief of the Roman Church? (ITRCH pg. 139)
1471	**Sixtus IV**	Issued a papal bull making the nephew and children of the popes Roman princes by right. This pope had two illegitimate children. He conspired with one of his sons to usurp the principality of Florence from the Medici family. He decided upon a plan of assassination to be committed by some priests during a mass. Two Medici brothers were stabbed while taking mass and killed. (ITRCH pg. 145)
1484	**Innocent VIII**	Fathered 16 children. (ITRCH pg. 146)
1491	**Alexander VI**	As Cardinal Borgia, he had a live-in mistress and produced several illegitimate children. He bought the papal throne and was labeled as anti-Christ by other Catholics. Apostolic succession? (ITRCH pg. 147)
1503	**Pius III**	Wanted to reform the morals of the Roman Church and was poisoned. (ITRCH pg. 149)

Abbreviation: ITRCH = *Is The Roman Church Holy?* by J. A. Henderson

YEAR	POPE	NOTABLE EVENTS OR CHARACTER
1513	**Julius II**	Threw the "Keys" to heaven and hell into the Tiber River, thereby rejecting the Roman Church's belief in Peter as their foundation for apostolic succession. His statement at the time was this: "From henceforth the popes shall only need the sword of St. Paul." What sword the Apostle Paul had I do not know. Scripture fails to disclose that Paul was ever armed. But Julius was clear, the Roman Church no longer needed Peter. This came from the mouth of an infallible pope as head of an infallible church. Clearly it means, to me, that from this point on (at least) the Roman Church can no longer claim apostolic succession, which is false anyway, but here they reject it. This is interesting as it was only a few years in front of the Council of Trent, which wrote the current Roman Church catechism. This catechism affirms apostolic succession. Now I ask you, what happened to the concept of infallibility? Clearly this is another case of jabberwocky. (ITRCH pg. 150)
1513	**Leo X**	John de Medici was elected pope when he appeared to be a dying man (faked it.) The motivation was that it would give the cardinals more time to make an acceptable choice. Leo, though, lived! He advertised throughout Europe that absolution for sins such as adultery, incest, bestiality, assassinations, and parricide could be purchased. Leo was an atheist (well weren't they all!) He was called a god and was addressed as "Your Divine Majesty." Luther's protest grew out of this man's sale of indugences. (ITRCH pg. 154)
1529	**Adrian VI**	Poisoned. (ITRCH pg. 172)
1534	**Paul III**	Had a family of illegitimate children and made one son, Guy, cardinal at age 15. (ITRCH pg. 177)

Abbreviation: ITRCH = *Is The Roman Church Holy?* by J. A. Henderson

YEAR	POPE	NOTABLE EVENTS OR CHARACTER
1549	**Julius III**	One of the popes reigning during the Council of Trent. Directed the council to disregard any reforms. He stated this about any reforms that might be adopted by the council: "So long as the papal authority remains unbroken, such concessions can easily be revoked." It is reported that he made his son cardinal at age 16 and that he, the pope, was almost always drunk. Further, it is reported that Julius III was a notorious sodomite and the son that he made Cardinal, may have not been his son, but of another "arrangement" with him. Dowling reports that he (the young person) was keeper of Julius's monkey. (see *History of Romanism* pages 511, 512 by J.J. Dowling) (ITRCH pg. 178)
1555	**Marcel II**	Poisoned after a 21 day reign. (ITRCH pg. 180)
1555	**Paul IV**	This pope had been the grand inquisitor at Rome. He made this statement: "Better to annihilate mankind, than permit it to continue in error." His given name was Caraffa. He was one of the Pope's legates to the Council of Trent. The current Catholic Catechism is from Trent and was compiled by those similar in character to this pope. (ITRCH pg. 185)
1559	**Pius IV**	This man was Cardinal de Medici and related to Catherine de Medici, Queen Mother of France. Pius IV was trained in the principles of the inquisition. His order concerning French Huguenots (Calvinists) was "take no Huguenot prisoner, but instantly kill everyone that should fall into his hands." This "celibate" pope had a numerous family and generally finished each day dead drunk. He ruled during six of the years of the Council of Trent. (ITRCH pg. 186)

Abbreviation: ITRCH = *Is The Roman Church Holy?* by J. A. Henderson

ESCAPE FROM PAGANISM

YEAR	POPE	NOTABLE EVENTS OR CHARACTER
1566	**Pius V**	He was the grand inquisitor before being named pope. He loved persecuting heretics (protestants). In a communication to Phillip of Spain, he said, "We must make them swim in a sea of blood!" Further, he conspired to have Queen Elizabeth 1 of England assassinated and planned the St. Bartholomew's Day Massacre in France. (ITRCH pg. 186)
1572	**Gregory XIII**	This pope carried out the St. Bartholomew's Day Massacre in which 100,000 French Huguenots were slaughtered in one day. The head of Admiral Coligny (a Huguenot and a cabinet member of the King of France's government) was sent to the pope by Catherine de Medici and her son King Charles IX. To celebrate, a mural was painted in the throne room of the Vatican, which still exists there. (ITRCH pg. 189)
		The heraldic insignia for this pope was the Red Dragon of the Book of Revelation, chapter 12, which identifies the Dragon as Satan. There is a stone image of this Dragon on Gregory's tomb. Further, coins and medals were struck to celebrate the massacre and he had the image of the Dragon and Satan cast into them. This pope identified himself, thereby, as a servant of Satan. Go to this site on the internet for information about this pope and the Dragon (www.aloha.net/"mikesch/dragon.htm).
1585	**Sixtus V**	Poisoned by the Jesuits. (ITRCH pg. 191)
1590	**Urban VII**	Poisoned by the Jesuits. (ITRCH pg. 192)
1592	**Innocent IX**	Poisoned two months after his election by the Spanish Cardinals that elected him. (ITRCH pg. 193)

Abbreviation: ITRCH = *Is The Roman Church Holy?* by J. A. Henderson

YEAR	POPE	NOTABLE EVENTS OR CHARACTER
1592	**Clement VIII**	Poisoned by the Jesuits for threatening to dissolve the Jesuit order. (ITRCH pg. 193)
1605	**Leo XI**	Poisoned by the Jesuits. (ITRCH pg. 193)
1655	**Innocent X**	Had as his mistress, his widowed sister-in-law. (ITRCH pg. 200)
1667	**Alexander VII**	Publicly declared himself to be an atheist. (ITRCH pg. 201)
1721	**Innocent XII**	Poisoned by the Jesuits. (ITRCH pg. 207)
1758	**Clement XIII**	Poisoned by the Jesuits. (ITRCH pg. 211)
1769	**Clement XIV**	Poisoned by the Jesuits. (ITRCH pg. 213)
1775	**Pius VI**	He was a drunk, accused of adultery and incest. He, perhaps, started the French revolution by sending in "legions of monks" when the French National Assembly passed a law requiring all ecclesiastics to take an oath of allegiance to France. The reign of terror grew out of this, as the pope instructed the ecclesiastics in France not to take the oath. (ITRCH pg. 214)
1800	**Pius VII**	The French revolution, sparked by popery, just about destroyed popery. The previous pope died in a French prison. Napoleon, though, needed a pope in order to be crowned Emperor with the crown of Charlemagne. After this, the pope was a puppet of Napoleon. After the fall of Napoleon this pope restored the Jesuits and condemned Bible societies. (ITRCH pg. 217)

Abbreviation: ITRCH = *Is The Roman Church Holy?* by J. A. Henderson

YEAR	POPE	NOTABLE EVENTS OR CHARACTER
1823	**Leo XII**	Revived the tortures of the inquisition. Approved of the "auto de fe" in Spain and Portugal. This was an act of public penance performed by condemned heretics, or rather performed upon them. They would be publicly tortured then executed. This was a religious service and the death of the heretic was a human sacrifice to their god, or gods. (ITRCH pg. 221)
1829	**Pius VIII**	This pope sanctioned the coronation and rule in Portugal of Don Miguel, who, taking power by force, banished 40,000 citizens, imprisoned 28,000, and beheaded or poisoned 1,123 victims. (ITRCH pg. 222)
1830	**Gregory XVI**	This pope had an apartment in the Vatican for his mistress. He fathered her seven children. His position on the reform of the church's morality is explained in his pastoral letter of 1832 "since the church is enlightened by the Holy Spirit, it is really absurd to urge upon her renovation and regeneration, as though she could be liable to defect or dullness." So, according to this pope, and the others on this list, I am assured that the Holy Spirit condoned and urged this pope and the others to live in sin and commit all manner of criminal acts. This is exactly what the "infallibility" position proclaims! This is damnable, big time! (ITRCH pg. 223)
1846	**Pius IX**	It was the age of revolution, liberty, and fraternity. Several countries were in revolt against monarchy. Garibaldi, in Rome, led the revolution against the monarch of Rome, who was this pope. Pius fled to the protection of the King of Naples and appealed to France, Austria, and others for aid. Garibaldi was defeated and Pius returned to the papal throne. The liberties of Rome were suppressed in blood. It was claimed for him that he was the third visible presence of Jesus Christ amongst us. (ITRCH pg. 224)

Abbreviation: ITRCH = *Is The Roman Church Holy?* by J. A. Henderson

YEAR	POPE	NOTABLE EVENTS OR CHARACTER
		As you will recall from the section of this book about the Roman Church World View, that this pope was guilty of kidnapping a six month old Jewish baby. Further, he was "beatified" by Pope John Paul II. This raises Pius IX to the position of a god and is to be "venerated" (means worshipped) by the faithful.
		Third visible presence indeed!
1878	**Leo XIII**	A tool of the Jesuits. The general of the Jesuits, the "black pope," was the real pope. Leo set up the idolatrous worship of Mary to the exclusion of Jesus Christ. He is the pope of the rosary, because he revived that pagan practice. (ITRCH pg. 233)
1903	**Pius X**	A Jesuit and the first pope of the 20th Century. He wanted to return to the practices of the 15th and 16th centuries. He condemned the reformation and Protestants for being "corrupters." He also stated that they were "—the most pestilential disease of heresy—a mob of seducers."
		It was during this pope's reign and from the Vatican, that FR. Marianus de Luca made this statement:
		"A good shepherd kills the wolves who attack the sheep. Heretics corrupting Catholics are wolves attacking sheep. Therefore the Catholic Church, as a good shepherd, ought to kill heretics."
		De Luca was canonist and theologian at the Gregorian University at the Vatican. This quote is from page 266 of *Is The Roman Church Holy?* De Luca made this statement with the approval of the Jesuit pope, Pius X. Again, since the church and the pope are infallible, this has to be the current sentiment of the Roman Church about Protestants, does it not? (ITRCH pg. 135)

Abbreviation: ITRCH = *Is The Roman Church Holy?* by J. A. Henderson

ISBN 142517128-1

Printed in Great Britain
by Amazon